THE ORIGIN AND DEVELOPMENT OF EARLY CHRISTIAN CHURCH ARCHITECTURE

By the same author

THE THEOLOGY OF WILLIAM BLAKE
DAILY LIFE IN THE EARLY CHURCH
Studies in the Church social history of the first five centuries

Mosaic in S. Pudenziana

THE ORIGIN
AND DEVELOPMENT OF
EARLY CHRISTIAN
CHURCH
ARCHITECTURE

J. G. DAVIES

SCM PRESS LTD
56 BLOOMSBURY STREET
LONDON

First published 1952

Printed in Great Britain by
The Camelot Press Ltd., London and Southampton

CONTENTS

[v]

LIST OF ILLUSTRATIONS
WITH THEIR SOURCES

LIST OF DIAGRAMS

PREFACE

ONE OF THE consequences of specialization in the field of art history during the present century is that while certain individual British scholars have made valuable contributions in the form of detailed studies of particular aspects of early Christian art, e.g. J. W. Crowfoot's examination of Palestinian churches, no one has attempted to present a general survey of the whole field. Handbooks of this kind were not uncommon in Victorian England, but since then, apart from the excellent but necessarily brief British Museum Guide, no one has endeavoured to collate the many new discoveries which have shed fresh light on the art of the early Church. It is true that the Byzantine period has been made familiar by the careful work of O. M. Dalton and D. Talbot Rice, but even here more recent research has provided further material which affects their conclusions, while the pre-Byzantine period as a whole continues to be neglected. This study is an attempt to fill a part of this gap—a part in so far as it is concerned only with the architecture of the first six Christian centuries.

After a brief survey of the early growth and development of Christianity in order to provide an historical and geographical background to the subject, the origin of the basilica is investigated and its general characteristics and different types are reviewed. Then follows an examination of the central type of architecture with its divers plans, round, octagonal and cruciform. In conclusion, after a description of the furniture and appointments of the church and of its adjoining buildings, a short and generalized account is given of the several forms which Christian architecture assumed in different countries.

It would be very rash, indeed entirely false, to claim that the conclusions reached are all assured. As year by year campaign of excavation succeeds campaign and new architectural complexes are laid bare, it is impossible to dogmatize about all the problems which have exercised the minds of archaeologists and art historians for generations. Yet this may be said, on the negative side numerous theories, which are still given currency in England (e.g. by liturgiologists, with their own special sphere of study, who yet require accurate knowledge of the architectural setting of worship and who must needs rely on ancient text books, unless they are to search continental journals at great length), may be shewn conclusively to be false. On the positive side, new theories based on fresh discoveries have come to the fore and may be tentatively accepted, and these theories are here presented for consideration.

This study is by no means exhaustive, and this is particularly true of the final section concerned with the architecture of the different countries, but reference to the bibliography will provide the reader with information of those specialized and detailed accounts, themselves containing further bibliographies, which serve to supplement this introductory essay—it can be called no more; yet it will, I trust, be conceded that in an ever-widening field the attempt to give a broad survey of the main discoveries, problems and possible solutions is not without justification.

J. G. D.

The University,
Birmingham.

ACKNOWLEDGMENTS

THE AUTHOR wishes to express his thanks to Mrs F. Sumner and B. T. Batsford Ltd., for permission to reproduce Plate II: to The Department of Art and Archaeology, Princeton University, for Plates III, IV, X, XIII and XV: to The Society for the Promotion of Hellenic Studies and B. T. Batsford Ltd., for Plate V: to Mr Bernard Bevan and B. T. Batsford Ltd., for Plate IX: to the British Academy, Mr J. W. Crowfoot and The Oxford University Press for Plate XI; and to The Yale University Art Gallery for Plate XIV.

He is also most grateful to Mr D. W. Oliver of the Department of Geography in the University of Birmingham for drawing the map; to his wife both for her assistance with the plans and for her criticism of many passages which otherwise would have remained obscure, and to the Student Christian Movement Press not only for accepting this work for publication but also for their painstaking care and attention in seeing it through the press.

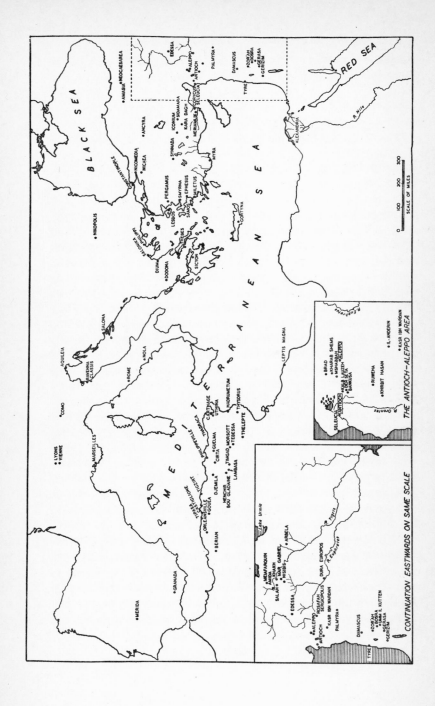

RED SEA

BLACK SEA

MEDITERRANEAN SEA

R. Nile

EDESSA
ALEPPO
PALMYRA
AMASIA
NEOCAESAREA
ANTIOCH
DAMASCUS
TYRE
ZORAH
BOSRA
GERASA
GERIZIM

ANCYRA
ICONIUM
SIDAMARA
KARA DAGH
MERIAMLIK
CORYCUS
SELEUCIA

NICOMEDIA
NICAEA
SYNNADA
MYRA
ALEXANDRIA

CONSTANTINOPLE
PERGAMUS
SMYRNA
EPHESUS
MILETUS
SAMOS
LESBOS

NIKOPOLIS

SALONICA
ITHOMI
THEBES
DIUMA
DODONA
SICYON
CORINTH
GORTYNA

SALONA
AQUILEIA
RAVENNA
CLASSIS
NOLA
ROME
LEPTIS MAGNA

COMO
CARTHAGE
UTHINA
HADRUMETUM
THYSDRUS
THELEPTE
TEBESSA

LYONS
VIENNE
MARSEILLES
PHILIPPEVILLE
HAIDRA
TIGZIRT
CIRTA
GUELMA
TIMGAD
MOROSOTT
LAMBASA
DJEMILA
TIPASA
CASTIGLIONE
ORLEANSVILLE
GOLEA
MENCHIR
BOU GLADANE
BERIAN

GRANADA

MERIDA

SCALE OF MILES
0   100   200   300

THE ANTIOCH–ALEPPO AREA

R. Euphrates
R. Orontes
SELEUCIA
ANTIOCH
BRAD
ANASAB SHEMS
MESHABBAH
AKBAR LAUZEH
KALOTEH
BANKUSA
RUWEHA
KHIRBIT HASAN
KASR IBN WARDAN
IL-ANDERIN

CONTINUATION EASTWARDS ON SAME SCALE

Lake Urmia
R. Tigris
R. Euphrates
MEIAFARQUIN
AMIDA
ZENARH
SUA GABRIEL
SALAH
NISIBIS
ARBELA
EDESSA
RESAFAH
HIERAPOLIS
DURA EUROPOS
KASR IBN WARDAN
ALEPPO
ANTIOCH
PALMYRA
DAMASCUS
TYRE
ZORAH
BOSRA
LAHA & KUTTEN
GERASA
GERIZIM

I

THE GEOGRAPHICAL AND
HISTORICAL BACKGROUND

THE HISTORY OF early Christian architecture can only
be fully appreciated in connexion with its geographical
distribution and that for three reasons. In the first
place, art is influenced by its surroundings, the form which
it takes in a particular region being in part dependent upon
its physical environment. In a wooded country, for example,
the architecture will be different from that in a district where
stone is easily quarried. In the second place, the geographical
position of certain towns helps to explain their pre-eminence
in the world of art. Thus Antioch, as a great port, not only
attracted visitors from Italy and Africa imbued with Greek
and Imperialist conceptions but also absorbed the ideas
which flourished in the hinterland and transmitted them to
the rest of the Mediterranean world. In the third place, it is
obvious that Christian art could only make its appearance
in those areas where there was to be found a nucleus of
believers, and it is *a priori* likely that in those provinces of
the Empire, and in those countries beyond its borders which
were first Christianized, there were to be found art centres of
vigour and originality which radiated their influences to
other parts still in the throes of conversion.

The first two of these factors fall into the sphere of what
Professor Talbot Rice has called 'art-study'[1] rather than into
that of art history, but references to them will be made as
occasion and space permits. Our immediate concern however
must be to trace the spread of Christianity from its beginnings
in Jerusalem to its acceptance in what St Paul calls 'all the

[1] *Vide* D. Talbot Rice, *The Background of Art*, 1939, pp. 13–27.

world', in order that the development of its architectural forms may be set against the geographical and historical background.

Much of the early history of the expansion of Christianity is unrecorded, and frequently the first reference to a local church represents it as a thriving community and provides no indication of how the faith was carried to that place nor of the patient work of consolidation, which must have taken not years but decades. This lack of information is noticeable from the outset of the missionary endeavour; thus Peter found believers at Joppa and Lydda in the coastal region of Judaea (Acts 9.32,36) and Saul at Damascus (9.19), but there is no previous mention of the Gospel being carried to any of these places. However, if details are not always forthcoming, the general picture is fairly clear in its broad outlines.

At Jerusalem James, the Lord's brother, took over the government of the church, but the Jewish-Christian mission of which this was the centre was not destined to enjoy a long period of development. The withdrawal to Pella in A.D. 70[1] and the final exclusion of all Jews from Aelia Capitolina, which was erected on the ruins of the Holy City after the Barcochba rebellion of 132, involved the failure of any attempt to create a Christian Israel after the flesh. Gentile Christians however soon settled there, under their bishop Marcus,[2] but, despite a certain amount of theological activity,[3] it was not until Constantine that Jerusalem recovered its position of importance; and indeed until then the local community was numerically so weak that it could not even obtain possession of the site of the holy sepulchre.[4]

The other localities in Palestine where bishops can be traced are Greek cities, although they did have a large non-Hellenic population. But even there Christians were in the minority and indeed several important towns such as Gaza refused to harbour them at all. On the sea coast, Christianity was to be found more among the floating population than

---

[1] Eusebius, H.E., iii. 5; Epiphanius, Haer., xxix. 7. [2] Eus., H.E., iv. 6.
[3] H.E., vi. 20. [4] Eus., Vita. Const., iii. 26.

among the natives[1], and even in matters spiritual it looked beyond the frontier to Alexandria; consequently its character was almost entirely Greek and before Constantine it is impossible to speak of Palestine being Christianized,[2] nor was the attempt made by the emperor and his successors to acclimatize the faith immediately successful, and as late as A.D. 400 many places were still essentially pagan. It follows that before the Peace of the Church there can have been little specifically Christian art in this area; here and there would be no doubt a few small churches, some mosaics and other products, but not much of importance and what there was would be Hellenistic and not the creation of indigenous artistic culture. After the Peace of the Church, however, Palestine began to exert considerable influence; pilgrims from all parts came to visit the Holy Places and naturally returned to their homes full of the glories of the magnificent basilicas and splendid mosaics, carrying with them as souvenirs little terra cotta flasks which bore designs of the treasures they had seen. In this way Palestine became a great diffusive centre, both absorbing and radiating diverse artistic currents.

To the north, in Syria, Christianity early gained a secure foothold and by the end of the first century it had been widely disseminated.[3] Antioch, the third city of the Roman Empire, numbered many believers amongst its population and indeed by the second half of the third century they were sufficiently influential for their bishop to be appointed as a high state official.[4] About the year A.D. 320, there were several churches in the city[5] and Chrysostom gives the total of those members attending the most important one as 100,000.[6] Antioch was the meeting place of several well-attended synods which took steps to deal with the Novatian schism and the heresy of Bishop Paul,[7] and the clergy were

---

[1] Eus., *Mart. Pal.*, iii. 3.
[2] cf. A. Harnack, *The Expansion of Christianity in the First Three Centuries*, 1905, II, p. 261.
[3] Ignatius, *Ad Philad.*, 10; *Didache*, 9, 10.
[4] Eus., *H.E.*, vii. 30.   [5] Theodoret, *H.E.*, i. 2.
[6] *In Mt. Hom.*, 85 (86), 4.   [7] Eus., *H.E.*, vi. 46; vii. 27f.

famous for their learning,[1] important schools being conducted by Malchion, Dorotheus and Lucian.[2] They were in touch with the churches of the eastern region of Asia Minor and with those of Alexandria and Rome and indeed Antioch itself, a great centre of Hellenic culture, was the chief intermediary between the East and the West, being connected with the former by land and with the latter by sea. Here traders from Anatolia, Persia and Armenia mingled with those from Gaul, Italy and Africa; here was the meeting place of Greek and oriental modes of expression, Iranian influences permeating from the north and Assyrian from Mesopotamia. From here came the inspiration of Ravennate art and one of the two great redactions of Gospel illustrations was Antiochene. No final assessment of the city's importance can yet be given because although literary sources describe certain of the buildings, such as the octagon of Constantine, excavation has so far been slow, as the modern town covers many of the remains.[3]

In the distinctively Syrian urban districts, Christianity spread from Edessa, the capital of Osrhoene in Mesopotamia, rather than from Antioch. It had been introduced before the mid-second century probably by Addai, a Palestinian Jew, who was subsequently confused with the apostle Thaddeus. At the turn of the century, the royal house, in the person of Abgar IX, joined the Church and Edessa became the headquarters of a missionary movement designed to convert Syria. It was to further this project that Tatian compiled his *Diatessaron*, a harmony of the four Gospels, and that Bardesanes (154–222), the boyhood friend of Abgar and a distinguished writer, engaged in his manifold activities to such good effect that there were bishops in all parts of Syria by the date of the Council of Nicaea. It was also from Edessa that the Gospel was carried further east to Nisibis, where a second theological school was founded, then to Amida, Arbela and Seleucia. The Aramaeans of these

[1] Jerome, *de vir.* ill., lxiv.   [2] Eus., *H.E.*, vii. 29, 32; ix. 6.
[3] *vide Antioch-on-the-Orontes, Publications of the Committee for the Excavation of Antioch and Its Vicinity,* 1934 onwards.

districts played a leading part in the development of Christian art. Through their schools at Edessa and Nisibis, and through the religious houses in Palestine and the West which contained many monks of Syrian origin, they compelled the recognition of oriental ideas and created the Syrian-Hellenistic art which came to fruition in the Byzantine period.

In Persia, the extensive persecution of the fourth century indicates the continued growth of Christianity, and further evidence is provided by Constantine's letter to King Sapur in which he declares: 'I am delighted to learn that the finest districts of Persia also are adorned with the presence of Christians.'[1] It was a Christianity unaffected as yet by Greek influence, as the homilies of Aphraates (337–45) clearly reveal. In the early fifth century, the Nestorians, suppressed within the Byzantine Empire, found a home in Persia and increasing rapidly they pushed further and further east even crossing the Oxus into inner Asia.

But the Christian country *par excellence* in the pre-Constantinian era was neither Persia nor even Syria but Asia Minor, where the expansion was from the first very swift. In the Greek cities along the coast and up the vallies, the missionaries, whose task had been facilitated by Jewish predecessors, encountered a form of Hellenism which was peculiarly susceptible to Christianity, and on the virgin soil of the hinterland, once the seat of the Hittite civilization of which traces survived in Christian buildings, they had no powerful national religion to overcome. The labours of St Paul had led to the establishment of some of the first Christian communities, and within fifty years of his death they were to be found in almost every province from Cicilia to Lydia,[2] and from Bithynia to Pontus.[3] In the second century they were strong enough to send missionaries to Gaul,[4] and by the time of the Council of Nicaea the whole country was covered by a network of bishoprics and the synodal and metropolitan

[1] Eus., *Vita Const.*, iv. 13.
[2] Ignatius, *Ad Philad.*, 11; Eus., *H.E.*, vi. 46; vii. 5.
[3] Pliny, *Ep.*, xviii.   [4] Eus., *H.E.*, v. 1.

consolidation of the Church, framed on the pattern of the local diets, had been completed. Ephesus was second only to Antioch as a Christian city, and along the coast such places as Smyrna, Miletus and Sardis were focuses of thriving religious life and thought. To the north-west, Proconessus, with its marble quarries and its export trade in columns and sculpture, attracted craftsmen from all quarters and played a leading part in the blending of styles. To the east in Cappadocia, Caesarea was famous for the scholastic labours of Alexander and Firmilian, the former being the friend of Clement and Origen and one time Bishop of Jerusalem, the latter being the correspondent of Cyprian. A seat of learning and a home of the monastic movement, it later produced Basil and the two Gregorys.

In the neighbouring province of Armenia Minor, Christians are first heard of in the middle of the third century, when Dionysius of Alexandria wrote to the brethren and to their bishop Meruzanes.[1] *The Testament of the Forty Martyrs of Sebaste* shows that by the time of the Licinian persecution the faith was widely diffused. During the same period the kingdom of Armenia was also penetrated, and Tiridates III was converted *c.* A.D. 280 through the efforts of Gregory the Illuminator, who, fleeing before the Persians, had embraced Christianity at Caesarea and, after ordination by its bishop Lentios, had returned to his native land. By 316, the year of the king's death, Armenia was mainly a Christian country.

In Pontus, which adjoins Armenia Minor on the north-west, the faith was firmly established at Amasia by the middle of the third century and its bishop consecrated Gregory Thaumaturgus to the see of Neocaesarea *c.* A.D. 240; in this town there were apparently seventeen Christians at the time of Gregory's elevation, but at his death some thirty years later there were reputed to be only that number of pagans.[2]

The four central provinces, Phrygia, Galatia, Pisidia and Lycaonia, produced no great bishops or writers, and there is

[1] Eus., *H.E.*, vi. 46.   [2] Gregory of Nyssa, *Vita.*

therefore little information of local church history. Nevertheless, Christianity was soon deeply entrenched, as may be
inferred from the growth of the Montanist movement[1] and
from the synods of Iconium and Synnada.[2] There is a similar
lack of knowledge about the three southern districts of
Isauria, Pamphylia and Lycia, but since they were able to
send twenty-five bishops to Nicaea the Christian population
must have been large and flourishing.

From Bithynia in the north, missionaries following in the
footsteps of St Paul crossed to Thrace and Moesia, and before
the fourth century there were many churches in existence in
what is now the modern Bulgaria maintaining relations with
Asia Minor. But in the south, apart from such centres as
Salonika and Corinth, Christianity did not at first become
acclimatized, although it had achieved a firm footing by the
fifth century, especially in Dalmatia, where a wealth of
inscriptions reveals a prospering community, and at Salona,
where there is a Christian cemetery dating from the very
beginning of the second century.

The foundation of Contantinople gave added importance
to the neighbouring provinces and drew artists and scholars
from all corners of the civilized world, while ships from the
Euxine and Aegean, caravans from Persia and traders from
western Europe brought their riches to the new capital. The
increasing flood of influences from the hinterland of Asia
Minor and of Syria descended upon the Hellenistic cities of
the eastern Mediterranean littoral and was borne onwards
to the Imperial City where the different ideas were sifted and
co-ordinated. The important part played by Constantinople
in the later phases of Christian art must not pass unrecognized, and its commanding geographical position, its political
prestige and its prodigious artistic activity must here be
acknowledged. Yet for several centuries before the New
Rome reached its zenith Old Rome had been the primary
focus of the Christian faith.

The church of Rome was founded by unknown missionaries at an early date and was already important when St

[1] Eus., *H.E.*, v. 16.   [2] *H.E.*, vii. 7.

Paul wrote to it. At the time of the Neronian persecution there were many Christians in the capital, so that Clement could compare them with an army,[1] and at the beginning of the second century Hermas could liken the church to a great tree overshadowing the whole earth.[2] Its members included not only the poor but many who were rich[3] and influential,[4] and, despite the recurrent but spasmodic persecutions, a steady advance was maintained to such good effect that Decius declared that he would rather have a rival emperor in Rome than a bishop.[5] At the synod A.D. 250–1, which Cornelius summoned to cope with the schisms consequent upon the emperor's repressive measures, there were present sixty Italian bishops, which suggests that throughout the country there were at least a hundred episcopal sees at that date. Shortly afterwards, Dionysius (259–68) set up parish churches and organized the dioceses under metropolitan authority, the former task being completed later by Marcellus (308).[6]

Information about the diffusion of Christianity in southern Italy is very slight, but the catacombs at Naples are evidence of an important community as early as the second century. Until the middle of the third century Greek was the official language of the Church, and in north Italy Hellenistic influences were very strong; its Christianity being based upon Sirmium, Salonika and Asia Minor. Oriental ideas found access through the ports of Classis and Aquileia which had trade relations with the head of the Adriatic and with the eastern Mediterranean, and at Ravenna all the bishops down to Peter (396–425) were of Syrian origin.[7]

The Greek population on the Mediterranean coast of Gaul and in the Rhone valley, where Christianity was established about the middle of the second century, was also in close touch with the East, as evidenced by the letter from Vienne and Lyons describing to the churches of Asia and

---

[1] *Ep.*, xxxvii.   [2] *Sim.*, viii. 3.   [3] *ibid.*, i. 1, 2.
[4] Ignatius, *Ad Rom.*, 4.   [5] Cyprian, *Ep.*, lv. 9.
[6] Duchesne, *Liber Pontificalis*, I, p. 157.
[7] Agnellus, *Liber Pontificalis ecclesiae Ravennatis*, xxiv.

Phrygia the persecution of A.D. 177.[1] In the western districts there was little Christianity before the fourth century, but by A.D. 314, the council of Arles, bishoprics had been created in all parts. It was not however until after A.D. 450 that Gaul, i.e. its Roman population, became substantially Christian.

There were also present at Arles, besides the native clergy, three bishops from Britain, but little is known of the previous history of the church there when it was no more than a military province with a veneer of Roman influence. It was only in the fourth century that Britain became Christianized to any large extent, and consequent upon the barbarian invasions it was cut off from the rest of Christendom in the middle of the next century; the last recorded British visit to Rome being made by St Patrick about 441 to obtain Leo's support for his mission to Ireland. In the interval which elapsed before the arrival of St Augustine, the Celtic church, stimulated by Druidic competition, became first in Wales and then in Ireland 'the rallying point of European intellectual life' and indeed it was its sturdy, independent vigour that was mainly responsible for the mission despatched by Gregory in 597.[2] Even distant Britain was subject to oriental influences, both Ninian the evangelist of the Scots in Galloway, and Patrick, the apostle of Ireland, having been trained in the monasteries of Gaul.

The history of the Spanish church begins, apart from a brief reference by Tertullian,[3] with the third century, when a letter from Cyprian reveals that there were Christians at Leon, Astorga, Merida and Saragossa.[4] By this period the faithful were already numerous, and their bishops formed a united synod. The only other source of information is the canons of the Council of Elvira (c. A.D. 303) which indicates that Christianity was widely diffused, and indeed the process of secularization which they were designed to check reveals a previous development of many years. Nothing is known of how the Gospel was first brought to Spain, but

[1] Eus., *H.E.*, v. 1f.
[2] T. Dayrell Reed, *The Rise of Wessex*, 1947, pp. 184–93.
[3] *Adv. Jud.*, vii.   [4] *Ep.*, lxvii. 1.

it is probable that it reached there almost as early as it reached Rome itself.

North-west Africa, the fertile strip of land between the sea and the range of mountains, was a second Italy and the granary of Rome. Next to nothing is known of the primitive Greek period of the African church, and Harnack's contention that its development was parallel to that in Asia Minor is by no means sure, for the cultured classes remained at first mainly hostile and pagan cults continued to attract large numbers of devotees. Nevertheless in Tertullian's day there were Christians in many parts, at Hadrumetum, at Thysdrus in Byzacium, at Lambasa and Uthina, at Carthage and in Mauretania[1] and in the next century the number of converts increased rapidly, so that at the synod under Agrippinus, *c.* 218–22, which discussed the validity of heretical baptism, there were present some seventy African and Numidian bishops,[2] while ninety bishops attended another synod at Lambasa under Cyprian's predecessor Donatus.[3] The Punic element in the church only became strong in the fourth century when both bishop and parish priest had to know the language, but the indigenous Berber population was hardly touched and this in part explains the almost total disappearance of Christianity after the later Mohammedan invasions. Before this onslaught, however, the province had already been overrun by the Arian Vandals, A.D. 429–39, but it was regained for Justinian by Belisarius in 535, and remained a Byzantine province until the end of the seventh century. Despite its commercial connexions with Rome, North Africa drew most of its architectural inspiration from the East, quite possibly via Egypt.

Although Eusebius records the legend of St Mark's mission,[4] and provides a list of bishops,[5] there is little reliable information of the history of Christianity in Egypt until the episcopate of Demetrius, at the end of the second century, when there was a flourishing catechetical school at Alexandria

[1] *Ad Scap.*, iii, iv; *De Monog.*, xii.
[2] Augustine, *De Bapt.*, ii. 8.   [3] *Ep.*, lix. 10.
[4] *H.E.*, ii. 16.   [5] *H.E.*, iii. 14, 21; iv. 1, 4, 5, 11, 19; v. 9, 22.

under the guidance of Pantaenus, who was succeeded first by
Clement and then by Origen.[1] Alexandria itself was a great
Hellenistic city, a centre of trade and culture and the chief
representative of Greek feeling in the graphic arts, the
influence of which is to be found as far afield as the Roman
catacombs. The record of the Decian and Valerian persecutions reveals a wide diffusion of Christianity in the third
century, and the presence of Christians in the remote villages
of the interior is shown by the *libelli* or certificates of having
sacrificed during the Decian persecution which have been
found among the Egyptian papyri.[2] By the time of Athanasius the episcopal organization had so far progressed that
there were nearly a hundred bishoprics in existence.[3]
Paganism had almost disappeared and the Scriptures were
translated into Coptic. Abyssinia with its capital at Axum was
Christianized in the sixth century at the instigation of the
Empress Theodora. The influence of the Coptic church
through Alexandria was considerable and the Desert Fathers,
living in solitude in the Natron Valley and the Thebaid,
were renowned throughout the civilized world, and were
prime movers in the development of monasticism.

During the early part of our period, Christians in all
these countries were liable to recurrent persecution, but the
frequency of these should not be exaggerated; they were
intermitted with quiet periods when the Church was free
from molestation and during which the work of evangelization could continue unimpeded by government interference. The most notable expansion took place in the fifty or
sixty years immediately prior to the Diocletian persecution,
and after his failure and the conversion of Constantine the
way lay open for a steady and rapid advance.

[1] Eus., *H.E.*, v. 10.

[2] H. M. Gwatkin, *Selections from Early Writers illustrative of Church History to the
time of Constantine*, 1914, p. 144; J. R. Knipfing, 'The Libelli of the Decian
Persecution,' *H.T.R.*, XVI, 1923, pp. 345–90.

[3] Athanasius, *Apol. c. Arian.*, 71.

c

II

THE BASILICA

IN THE EARLY days of the Church Christian worship was essentially a private activity and although for a time Jewish Christians continued to take part in the services of the Temple and of the synagogues, the 'breaking of bread' was confined to the house of one of the faithful, and all non-believers were rigidly excluded. In the West, where the evangelization of the pagans lagged behind that in the East, the private house continued in use for some considerable time, references to it being made, for example, by Justin Martyr at his trial[1] and by Gregory of Tours who records how one Leocadius, in the middle of the third century, gave his house to the church at Bourges.[2] Even in North Africa in the fourth century, a small congregation like that at Cirta continued to have its liturgical assemblies in the home of one of its members. But where the missionary endeavour was more successful the domestic character of the primitive Eucharist tended to become obscured, because in those parts where there was a flourishing community, too large to be accommodated in a single dwelling place, it became necessary to erect special buildings for worship. It was only where and when these conditions arose that Christian architecture came into existence.

The popular idea that during the first three centuries Christianity was under such continuous persecution that its adherents were driven to worship in secrecy in the catacombs and other hiding places does not conform with the facts. Christianity was at first a *religio illicita*, a religion unrecognized by the law, and its professors were liable at any time to be haled before the magistrates; their position was therefore

[1] *Acta Just. et Soc.*, ii.   [2] *Hist. Fr.*, i. 29.

admittedly precarious but, apart from isolated outbreaks of mob violence and a limited number of authorized persecutions, they were left to practise their beliefs without interference.

The persecutions which were carried out under imperial orders were not many, and in the aggregate occupied a very small part of the three centuries over which they extended. The persecution of Nero in A.D. 64 was limited to Rome itself and that of Domitian (81–96), if it ever took place,[1] was of short duration. Under Trajan (97–117) there were scattered popular risings against the Church, but the emperor's policy was one of moderation and he restrained his officials from excessive measures. Marcus Aurelius (161–80) issued an edict condemning Christians, and the letter of the churches of Lyons and Vienne[2] witnesses to an intensive local persecution, but apart from a sporadic outburst towards the end of the reign of Septimius Severus (193–211) and under Maximin (235–8), the Church was spared a serious attempt to extirpate the faith until Decius (249–51). His action was however directed chiefly against the clergy and it did not last more than a year. The persecution was resumed under Valerian (253–60) but was suspended by Gallienus (261–8), who restored those churches which had been confiscated and allowed freedom of worship. During the first twenty years of the reign of Diocletian (284–305) the emperor was favourably disposed towards the Church, even employing Christians as his personal servants, but under the influence of Galerius the last and most bloody persecution began, being finally brought to an end in the West by Constantine's victory at the Milvian Bridge in 312, and in the East by his triumph at Adrianople twelve years later. It is obvious from this brief outline that the Church enjoyed long periods of peace when it was free to assemble without subterfuge and also, as its numbers increased, to build churches and to erect chapels and monuments in its cemeteries. Under these circumstances it is only to be

[1] *vide* R. L. P. Milburn, 'The Persecution of Domitan', *C.Q.R.*, CXXXIX, 1945, pp. 154–64.
[2] Eus., *H.E.*, v. 1–3.

expected that evidence of Christian architecture before
Constantine should be forthcoming and indeed the edicts
which brought these conflicts to an end all expressly com-
mand the restoration of church buildings to the Christians—
that of Galerius in 311,[1] that of Maximin in 313[2] and that
of Licinius in the same year.[3]

In the East, beyond the Tigris, evidence of Christian
architecture is to be found as early as the second century, for
the *Chronicle of Arbela*, written by Mesihazekha *c.* A.D. 550
and based upon the record of Abel (A.D. 171–*c.* 200), records
that the third bishop Isaac (123–36) was responsible for the
building of a church. *The Chronicle of Edessa* also provides the
information that there was in the city a *templum ecclesiae
Christianorum* which was destroyed by a flood in A.D. 202.
At Dura-Europos on the Euphrates, where the local congregation was not wealthy, a private house was transformed,
c. 232, into a Christian place of worship by removing a
partition between two rooms and by furnishing another as
a baptistery. In Pontus, Gregory Thaumaturgus built a
church at Neocaesarea in 258; twelve years later the emperor
Aurelian ordered Paul of Samosata to surrender the 'church-
building' at Antioch to the orthodox party[4] and at the turn of
the century Gregory the Illuminator directed the construction of three basilicas at Etchmiadzin. At Nicomedia, the
Eastern capital itself, the church was situated on rising ground
in full view of the imperial palace, and when Diocletian ordered
its destruction it had to be pulled down, as any attempt to
fire it would have endangered the surrounding buildings.[5]

In the West, despite the slow spread of Christianity,
Tertullian bears witness to the existence of church buildings
in the second century, some of them being quite elaborate
structures,[6] and after the Peace Constantine gave the clergy

---

[1] Eus., *H.E.*, viii. 17.　　[2] *ibid.*, ix. 10.　　[3] Lact., *De Mort. Persec.*, xlviii.
[4] Eus., *H.E.*, vii. 30.　　　　　　[5] Lact., *op. cit.*, xii.
[6] *De Spect.*, xxv; *De Pudic.*, iv; *De Idol.*, vii. The statement of Minucius Felix
that Christians had no 'temples' (*Octavius*, xxxii) does not conflict with this, for
his meaning was that they had no places where carnal sacrifices were offered;
the same statement is made by both Arnobius (*Adv. Gent.*, vi. 1) and Lactantius
(*Inst.*, ii. 2.) writing at a time when there were many churches in use.

[14]

of North Africa sufficient money to rebuild those which had been destroyed. In the provinces of Gaul and Britain, under Diocletian, Constantius 'lest he should have seemed to dissent from the injunctions of his superiors, permitted the demolition of churches—mere walls, and capable of being built up again—but he preserved entire that true temple of God, which is the human body.'[1] In Rome itself, during the reign of Alexander Severus (222–35), there was a dispute between the Christians and the guild of *popinarii* concerning the ownership of a plot of land upon which the Christians intended to build a church and the guild a public-house. The emperor decided in favour of the Christians on the grounds that the worship of God in any form was better than the licence of a tavern.[2] The church erected on this site, which according to tradition was consecrated by Callistus, was no doubt one of those restored by the rescript of Gallienus, which although not giving Christianity the position of a *religio licita*, must have stimulated the growth and development of Christian architecture, and according to the report of Optatus of Milevis there were more than forty basilicas in Rome by the beginning of the fourth century.[3] Indeed by this time there had been such progress that Eusebius was led to ask: 'How could one fully describe those assemblies thronged with countless men, and the multitudes that gathered together in every city, and the famed concourses in the places of prayer; by reason of which they were no longer satisfied with the buildings of olden times, and would erect from the foundations churches of spacious dimensions throughout all the cities?'[4]

Thus before the fourth century, in both the eastern and western halves of the Empire and beyond its borders, Christians were in the habit of meeting for worship no longer in private houses but in large buildings especially constructed for the purpose. Few traces however of these churches remain, so that there is little direct evidence of the forms

[1] Lact., *De Mort. Persec.*, xv.   [2] Lampridius, *Vita. Alex.*, xlix.

[3] *De Schism. Donat.* ii. 4.   [4] *H.E.*, viii. 1.

which they took.[1] From the Constantinian period, however, there is an abundance of information which indicates that the basilica was by then the predominant type. Its origin is, however, obscure precisely because of the dearth of archaeological data from the time during which it was developed.

The facile solution once adopted by scholars that the basilica was the invention of one of the architects of the emperor Constantine fails to take account of the continuity of art. General histories of art tended to divide the subject into a series of unconnected great ages, and there was no recognition that the style of a particular epoch has grown out of what has preceded it without any violent or immediate break. The Christian basilica as it first appears under Constantine was already complete and remained in use with little modification for the next four centuries. Its main features were: a rectangular room, divided into three sections by two rows of columns parallel with the longer side; the entrance was in one of the shorter sides, opposite to a semicircular niche in the other; the roof covering the nave was higher than that over the side aisles thus providing window space to illuminate the building. Such creations as this do not spring suddenly into existence, they are the fruit of long periods of steady growth and experiment, and the origin of the basilica lies not in the genius of an individual architect but in the joint endeavours of both pagans and Christians in the first three centuries of the Church's history.

The suggestion that the basilica derived from the *schola*[2] has nothing to support it, except for St Paul's visit to one at Ephesus (Acts 19.9), since what little is known of the ancient school building indicates that it did not conform to any one type and in no case had any great resemblance to its supposed architectural descendent. Nor is it true to say that the private basilica had a determinative influence on Christian

---

[1] According to L. H. Vincent and E. M. Abel (*Emmaus, sa basilique et son histoire*, 1932) the basilica which they have excavated at 'Amwas dates from the early third century, but this contention has been devastatingly criticised by J. W. Crowfoot (*Palestine Exploration Fund Quarterly Statement*, January, 1935, pp. 40 ff.) and by J. Lassus (*Sanctuaires chrétiens de Syrie*, 1947, pp. 80–7).

[2] G. Baldwin Brown, *From Schola to Cathedral*, 1886.

architecture, for apart from those in the imperial palaces, which could hardly have been used without the cognizance of the emperor, they were few in number[1] and there is no certainty that they followed a uniform plan. De Rossi's solution is equally unacceptable; he derives it from the *cellae cimiteriales*, small chapels built above the catacombs and all possessing an apse; but these are really miniature basilicas and the question remains unanswered. The once widely accepted theory, however, which has received new publicity in a recent book,[2] that it developed from the private dwelling has more to recommend it. A congregation which was accustomed to worship in the chief room of a house would not be likely to make many changes when the property was put exclusively at their disposition, and even in the construction of a new building it is reasonable to suppose that they would adhere to the familiar plan.[3]

The chief room of the old Roman house was the *atrium*, a rectangular apartment surrounded by small chambers and covered with a single gable roof (*testudinatum*). Access was obtained to it from the street by means of the porch (*vestibulum*) and the entrance hall (*ostium*), opposite which was the *tablinum*, a recess containing the family records and archives as well as the sacred hearth and the altar of the household gods. On either side of the tablinum was a small room; these wings (*alae*) contained the ancestral portraits (*imagines clypeatae*), and extended to the outer walls of the house, which were pierced to provide light. In crowded districts these windows were insufficient and so a rectangular opening was made in the centre of the roof. The roof itself sloped down towards the opening so that the rain ran into a cistern (*impluvium*) in the middle of the atrium floor. Between this basin and the tablinum stood a stone table (*cartibulum*), a relic of the primitive chopping block, later used for vases of flowers.

[1] cf. *Recog. Clem.*, X. lxxi, where however the Latin translator may have introduced the word 'basilica'.

[2] G. Dix, *The Shape of the Liturgy*, 1945, pp. 22-7.

[3] *vide* W. Lowrie, *Christian Art and Archaeology*, 1901, pp. 95ff.

The Greek peristyle, on the other hand, was an open court surrounded on three sides by a covered colonnade around which various chambers, such as the banqueting hall (*triclinium*), were disposed. Facing the narrow passage (*thuroreiov*) communicating with the front door was the *prostas* which corresponded to the Roman tablinum and similarly contained the altar.

It is alleged that during the first centuries of the Christian era one type of house was in predominant use being reproduced time and time again with only insignificant variations; this was the Roman plan, extended and modified under Greek influence by combination with the peristyle. It was from this building, according to many of the old school of archaeologists, that the Christian basilica developed, and indeed the similarity of plan is quite striking, especially when compared with certain houses excavated at Pompeii. Hence the tablinum, which had been the family shrine and the place where the paterfamilias had his seat at the meeting of the clan, became the apse where the bishop sat on his cathedra surrounded by his presbyters; the cartibulum was transformed into the altar and the alae were adopted as transepts, their decoration with ancestral portraits inspiring the medallions of the popes, while the impluvium was used for ablutions and for the solemn administration of baptism.

Prima facie this theory carries conviction, but further examination reveals certain objections which must be deemed fatal. In the first place, the roofing of the atrium was entirely different from that of the basilica. Vitruvius distinguishes five kinds of atrium. The testudinatum, with single gable roof and no opening, gave way at an early date to the *tuscanicum*, in which the roof was supported by four beams, crossing each other at right angles, the rectangular space included by the beams being left open. A development of this was the *tetrastylum* in which the main beams of the roof were supported by pillars placed at the four corners of the rain-water tank; the *corinthium* was constructed according to the same principle, the only difference being that there was a greater number of pillars around the cistern. Finally there

was the *displuviatum,* which had its roof sloping away from the
cistern, so that the rainwater was not conducted towards the
central opening in the roof but fell outside the house. No
simple modification of any of these arrangements would
produce interior arcades, high walls and a clerestory, and it
must therefore be concluded that the private house was not
the source of these most characteristic features of the basilica.
The second objection to this theory is that the tablinum was
rectangular whereas the apse, especially in Rome, was usually
semicircular. The disposition of the sanctuary may well have
been due to the influence of the private house, but the form
it assumed must obviously be derived from elsewhere.
Thirdly, the alae were much larger in dimension than the
transepts, which in any case scarcely appear in basilicas
outside Rome itself and were therefore not indispensable
constituents of the usual plan. Fourthly, and more important
still, the allegation that one form of house was universally
adopted in the first centuries of the Christian era, while no
doubt not unreasonable as long as the remains at Pompeii
were the only evidence at the disposal of the archaeologist,
is no longer tenable in view of the extreme diversity of types
which have been discovered in the last fifty years. Admittedly
other examples of the Greek house with peristyle, of the
Roman house with atrium and of the combination of the two
have been found, but there are also the tenement houses of
Rome and Ostia with shops on the ground floor and several
storeys above; there are the farms of Gaul and North Africa
of which scarcely a single one resembles another; there are
the houses of Timgad and Djemila whose resemblance to
those of Pompeii and Herculaneum is anything but close. In
the East and particularly in Syria, the variety is even greater;
at Antioch and Seleucia excavations have revealed a profusion of different plans, from the small ones with diminutive
rooms connected by corridors to the large ones with rooms
placed in a line one behind the other with no means of direct
communication between them.[1] To assert that the church of
the early Christians was a private house is to affirm that it

[1] J. Lassus, *op. cit.,* p. 4.

had a different plan in Rome from what it had in Africa and that in Antioch it assumed ten dissimilar forms.

Finally, reference must be made to those few examples of a house-church which have been discovered in recent years. In Rome excavations have been carried out beneath the *tituli*, the parish churches, and in particular beneath the basilicas of St Clement, St Anastasia, SS John and Paul and St Martin. The present St Clement's stands above the primitive fourth-century edifice which it replaced when it was destroyed in 1084 by the Normans of Robert Guiscard. At a lower level still there are two houses, the one under the nave consisting of warehouses on the ground floor and above these a number of rooms where the church assembled for worship.[1] At St Anastasia likewise the congregation was installed on the first floor above a row of shops,[2] while the *titulus* of SS John and Paul occupied the whole building, the upper room being set apart for the celebration of the liturgy, and those beneath, one of which has frescoes depicting scenes of martyrdom, being used for a variety of purposes including the storing of wine for the Eucharist. The house-church excavated in the proximity of St Martin's, in the fourth century the *titulus Sylvestri* and in the third the *titulus Equitii*, had a rectangular assembly hall on the ground floor which was entered by a vaulted vestibule.[3] It is in the East, however, that the most complete example of a house-church has been preserved, namely the one at Dura-Europos which was constructed at the beginning of the third century. Access from the street is obtained by a single entrance door in the north wall which opens into a vestibule and thence into the court. On the east side of the court there is a portico and along the other three five rooms are disposed (*Fig. 1*). In the north west corner is the baptistery,[4] richly decorated with frescoes, its font

---

[1] E. Junyent, *Il titolo di San Clemente in Roma*, 1932.   [2] *ibid.*, p. 32.

[3] R. Vielliard, *Les origines du titre de Saint-Martin-aux-Monts à Rome*, 1931.

[4] When the building was first excavated the purpose of this room was disputed. C. Hopkins considered the niche at one end to be a font and the room therefore to be a baptistery, while P. V. C. Baur believed the niche to be a reliquary and the room the place of assembly for worship (*The Excavations at Dura-Europos, conducted by Yale University and the French Academy of Inscriptions*

surmounted by a baldachin. Opposite to this, along the southern wall of the house, two rooms have been made into one, at the east end of which there is a small platform for the altar and a door to the side of it leads into what was

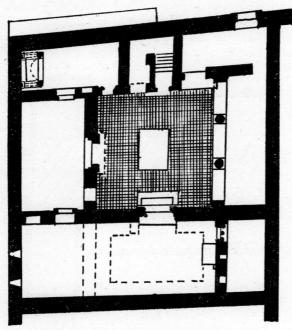

Fig. 1. House-church, Dura-Europos.

originally the sacristy. The use of the other room along the west wall is doubtful, but graffiti suggest that it was employed either as a triclinium or as a class room for the catechumens. All these examples of house-churches, however they may differ in disposition, have this in common—that no use was made of the court or atrium for the purpose of worship; the congregation gathered in a special room, either downstairs or on the first floor depending upon the arrangement and size

and Letters, 5th Season, 1934, pp. 249–55). It is the former theory that is now generally accepted: cf. H. Grégoire, 'Les Baptistères de Cuicul et de Doura', *Byzantion*, XIII, 1938, pp. 589–93; Lassus, *op. cit.*, pp. 14f., 218.

of the house at their disposal. It is then necessary to pursue the enquiry further and in particular to examine the two most recent theories that have been propounded, viz. those associated with the names of E. Dyggve and J. Sauvaget.

Excavations at Marusinac, a suburban necropolis near Salona, have brought to light a funeral basilica which is hypaethral, i.e. without any roof over its centre; this is the first example to be discovered of a type of building already

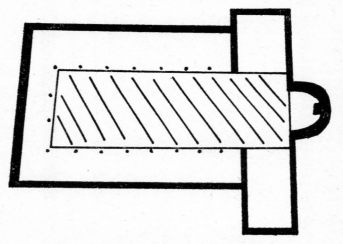

Fig. 2. Funeral basilica, Marusinac.

known from the texts as *basilica discoperta* or *ecclesia sine tecto*. It consists of an apse preceded by a tomb and opening on to a long open air court flanked by colonnades (*Fig. 2*). The similarity to the normal Christian basilica, if the centre space be roofed, is insisted on by Dyggve. Noting that the early Christians assembled in an ordinary room, without apse, he asserts that the penetration of the funeral liturgy into the parish church brought with it of necessity its usual accompaniments. The tomb became the altar and the seats placed around the tomb for the funeral meal became the presbyterium where the clergy had their place; and so by the fusion of these two architectural types the Christian basilica

of the fourth and fifth centuries came into existence.[1] This
is to base a weighty conclusion upon very little evidence, and
the evidence such as it is does not suffice to explain several
features, such as the clerestory and the gable roof, typical
of the classical Christian basilica. Moreover the axis of the
building at Marusinac is circular, i.e. on entering one is led
by the colonnades either to the right or left around the open
court, whereas the axis of the basilica is central, i.e. there is
a direct line from the door to the apse so that on entering one
is almost drawn, as it were, directly to the altar.[2] In any case
Marusinac remains an isolated example since the only other
known funeral basilica, that of Junius Piso at Mactar in
Tunisia, was not hypaethral. This building was originally
constructed in A.D. 93 as a meeting place for the *juvenes* of
Mactar and it was provided with a gymnasium (*palaestra*) in
front of its principal doorway.[3] The palaestra was in the form
of an open court with colonnades along at least three of its
sides, while the main building had three aisles and a semicircular projecting apse. It was not until later, at the time of
the Severuses, that Julius Piso was buried in the porch and
the tomb of his daughter Julia Spesina was placed beneath a
baldachin in front of the apse. Hence, while admitting the
general similarity to the Christian basilica, it cannot be
taken as a true example of a pagan funeral basilica since it
was not used as such until some considerable time later,
being built for an entirely different purpose.[4] Since the apse
of the basilica of Lucila Stratonice at Lyons, another funeral

[1] E. Dyggve and R. Egger, *Forschungen in Salona*, III, 1939, pp. 80–106;
E. Dyggve, 'Probleme des altchristlichen Kultbaus, Einige archäologisch
begründete Gesichtpunkte zu Grabkult und Kirchenbau', LIX, 1940, pp.
103–13).

[2] It must however be admitted that in those churches where the arrangement
of the faithful was longitudinal and the central portion of the nave was left
empty (*vide postea*, p. 38) there was an approximation to a circular axis.

[3] G. Picard, 'La basilique funéraire de Julius Piso à Mactar', *Comptes rendus
de l'Académie des Inscriptions et Belles-Lettres*, 1945, pp. 185–212; 'Fouilles de
Mactar', *Bulletin archéologique du Comité des Travaux historiques et scientifiques*,
February 1947, pp. xx–xxvii.

[4] The basilica was eventually taken over by Christians, who chiselled away
the reliefs on the tomb of Julia and provided the apse with a synthronus and
cathedra.

basilica, is so far the only part of the building to have been traced,[1] it is impossible to adduce it as reliable evidence, beyond acknowledging that it demonstrates, what was already known from inscriptions,[2] that there were funeral basilicas in existence. Their influence on Christian architecture is almost impossible to assess; certainly the evidence so far does not warrant their being regarded as the immediate prototype of the so-called Constantinian basilica; that there was some relationship seems not unlikely, but that relationship, it will be argued below, consisted not in their being in the same line of evolution but in their both springing from the same ancestor yet developing independently.

Dyggve has found a further example of a hypaethral basilica in the palace of Theodoric at Ravenna, and this leads him to seek the origin of the Christian basilica in the audience chambers and throne rooms of the imperial residences.[3] In St Apollinare Nuovo at Ravenna there is a mosaic depicting a large structure inscribed PALATIUM. It has been usual to interpret this as a representation of the façade of Theodoric's palace, but the Danish scholar has argued conclusively that it is in fact the interior, the four sides being presented to the spectator together in accordance with a common artistic convention. Thus understood, the mosaic shows an open court with porticos surmounted by tribunes flanking the two long sides; of the shorter sides one is a simple wall pierced by a door, while the other is a *tetrakionion*, here a triple arch beneath a pediment. It is therefore a hypaethral basilica with three aisles. It has some resemblance to the peristyle in Diocletian's palace at Spalato, at the same time as having certain affinities with the palace of the exarchs at Ravenna. Since the throne room was situated behind this court, the whole complex consisted of three parts, viz. a hypaethral basilica with a monumental doorway (the

[1] W. Seston and C. Perrat, 'Une basilique funéraire païenne à Lyon', *Revue des Etudes Anciennes*, XLIX, 1947, pp. 139–59.

[2] *C.I.L.*, X, 3110.

[3] E. Dyggve, *Ravennatum palatium sacrum. La basilica ipetrale per cerimonie. Studii sull' architettura dei palazzi della tarda antichità*, 1941.

tetrakionion) at one end which led into the throne room itself. The analogy with Christian architecture, according to Dyggve, is evident, there being a close parallel to the atrium, the monumental doorway and the church proper. While accepting, without further question, this interpretation of the mosaic, it is difficult to see how this necessarily involves the conclusion that here is the origin of the Christian basilica. It is hardly logical at one moment to stress the analogy, according to which the open court corresponds to the atrium, and at the same time to say that the open court is the prototype of the basilica; if the analogy is to be preserved then the basilica must be derived from the throne room and the mosaic gives no clue to its form whatsoever.[1]

Dyggve has however received support independently from the French scholar Sauvaget who, setting out to discover the architectural origins of the Mohammedan mosque, has arrived at the conclusion that both mosque and basilica derive from the audience chamber of the imperial palaces. Arguing that the term 'basilica' applies not to a specific type or plan but to the function or usage of the building, he affirms that it was adopted from the *basileus*, the supreme ruler of the period, the oriental Hellenistic monarch who succeeded Alexander. 'Basilica' then would apply to some part of the palace of the basileus, and this, in view of its later form, could only be the open court surrounded by colonnades where justice was administered. The influence of Constantine is then postulated and he is deemed responsible for inducing the Church to adopt the audience chamber. The influence of the imperial cultus also led to the incorporation of the apse into the building, henceforward to serve as the sanctuary, the altar replacing the throne or statue. Hence it was the audience chamber of the imperial palace, elaborated by Roman architects from an oriental prototype which was the model for the Christian basilica.[2] Obviously this theory is

---

[1] The peristyle at Spalato has of course a circular axis, not a central one as at Ravenna.

[2] J. Sauvaget, *La mosquée omeyyade de Médine, Etude sur les origines architecturales de la mosquée et de la basilique*, 1947, p. 184.

mainly speculation and the known monuments do not provide a sufficient basis for accepting it. The importance attributed to Constantine is an interesting hypothesis with no shred of evidence, literary or otherwise, to support it. Above all, a hypaethron and a roofed building are, whatever may be said, two distinct types of architecture, each with its own independent line of development.

The inadequacy of these theories, both old and new so far reviewed, prompts the consideration of those buildings for which the generic term 'basilica' was already employed before its application to Christian churches. These civil basilicas served as courts of law and exchanges during the closing years of the Republic and under the Empire. In the West none of these edifices was erected before the end of the third century B.C., for Livy expressly states that there were no basilicas at the time of the fire which destroyed so many buildings in the forum under the consulate of Marcellus and Laevinus in 210 B.C.[1] In 184 however, the basilica Porcia was constructed, to be followed ten years later by one on the *clivus capitolinus*—henceforth basilicas became not uncommon. Despite considerable diversity in secondary detail, there were, according to Leroux,[2] from the beginning two main types of civil basilica:

A. A building whose width was greater than its length; examples of which are the basilica Julia erected in 155 B.C. and the Ulpian basilica constructed in the reign of Trajan in A.D. 114 (*Fig 3*).

B. A building whose length was greater than its width, for example the basilica at Tipasa (*Fig. 4*).

The first of these two types is undoubtedly of oriental origin, the main influence being that of Egypt where the transverse plan was from an early date the typical architectural form issuing in the hypostyle of which the famous room at Delos is an outstanding example.[3] The second type

[1] XXVI. xxvii. 3.
[2] G. Leroux, *Les origines de l'édifice hypostyle*, 1913, pp. 280ff.
[3] G. Leroux, *Exploration archéologique de Délos*, II, *La salle hypostyle*, 1904.

I. S. Apollinare Nuovo, Ravenna

II.   S. Apollinare in Classe, Ravenna

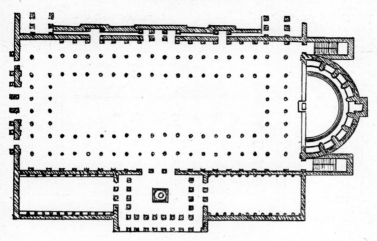

Fig. 3. The Ulpian basilica.

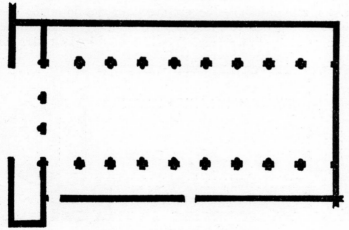

Fig. 4. Civil basilica, Tipasa.

of civil basilica preserves the central axis and main features of narrow oblong Greek *naos* or temple. The naos itself derived ultimately from the *megaron* or house (νάος and οἶκος were primitively synonymous), and consisted of the *cella*, which was the core of the building, being a reproduction of the

D   [27]

private dwelling, and the peristyle. Since the interior of the temple became of less and less importance, as it was not used for assemblies, the inside colonnades which carried the roof were either suppressed or merged into the outside walls; but

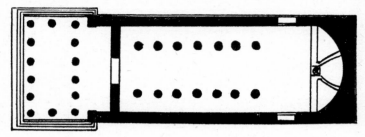

Fig. 5. The Telesterion, Samothrace.

in the great assembly halls and in those temples where the cult required space sufficient to accomodate a large number, e.g. for an initiation, the architectural development continued unimpeded to produce such buildings as the Telesterion at Samothrace (*Fig. 5*), which has obvious affinities

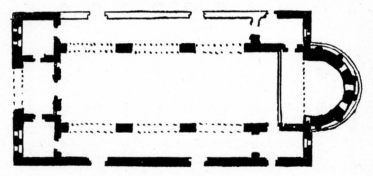

Fig. 6. Church of Kalb Lauzeh.

with the later civil basilicas at Rome and elsewhere. At Rome indeed throughout the last two centuries B.C. and later there was one single building that exercised a predominant influence on architectural style and that was the *curia oblonga*, the meeting hall of the senate, which was little else than a Greek naos with a narrow façade. This dependence upon Hellenistic inspiration and models continued for many centuries and the curia with which Diocletian replaced the one which had been destroyed in A.D. 305 was also of the oblong Greek form.

Hence while the Jewish synagogue may be derived from

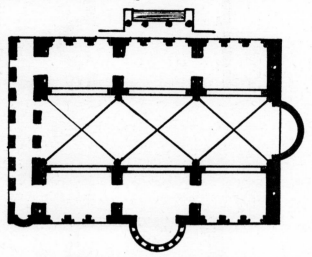

Fig. 7. The basilica of Maxentius, Rome.

type A, the Christian basilica has close affinities with type B, its main features, listed above, being clearly discernible. Indeed a comparison between Christian and civil basilicas reveals frequently almost an identity which, apart from other indications, would make it quite possible to mistake one for the other.[1] Thus the church at Kalb Lauzeh (*Fig. 6*) in Syria follows the same plan as that of the basilica of Maxentius[2] in the forum at Rome, and although the latter is vaulted

---

[1] There is however no reason to suppose that any great number of civil basilicas were transferred to the Church, since the social and commercial activities for which they were constructed continued unaffected by the triumph of Constantine.

[2] cf. with this the Frigidaria of the Baths of Diocletian. J. B. Ward-Perkins, 'The Italian Element in Later Roman and Early Mediaeval Architecture', *Proceedings of the British Academy*, 1947, p. 171.

there is little to distinguish them (*Fig. 7*). Similarly the
chapel of the monastery at Umm il-Ḳuṭṭin (*Fig. 8*) is in all
essentials like the temple of Apollos Pythios at Gortyna
(*Fig. 9*).[1] Indeed pagan precedents can be found for almost

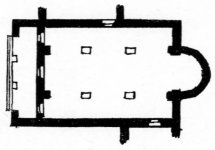

Fig. 8. Chapel of Umm il-Ḳuṭṭin.

every type of church erected during the Constantinian period
and later[2] and so the Christian basilica can be classified as a
direct descendent of the civil basilica, itself deriving from the
Greek temple. Hence also the gable roof, an invariable

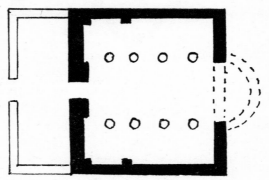

Fig. 9. Temple of Apollos Pythios, Gortyna.

feature of the naos and of its prototype, the megaron.[3] The
clerestory on the other hand, was not a Hellenistic creation

[1] See further the comparative tables in Leroux, *op. cit.*, pp. 316, 317.
[2] H. C. Butler, *Early Churches in Syria*, 1929, pp. 12–17.
[3] E. B. Smith, 'The Megaron and its Roof', *A.J.A.*, XLVI, 1942, pp. 99–118.

but came from Egypt,[1] as its other common descriptive title, Egyptian lighting, clearly demonstrates. The clerestory had already been incorporated into the civil basilica before the classic era of Christian architecture e.g. in the Basilica Julia and in the basilica of Maxentius.

Thus the emergence of the Christian basilica is seen as the result of an age-long development in which there were numerous stages, the final link in this chain of evolution being the civil basilica conforming to type B. Alternative theories tend to neglect the continuity of art in the quest for the immediate prototype, the discovery of which only presents the further problem of its ancestry and so a regressive process is initiated. The explanation which is here accepted begins at the other end and traces the style from its inception to its florescence in the Christian church.

This, in its essentials is the theory advanced so ably by G. Leroux. But while it may now count numerous adherents,[2] there are still those who continue to reject it.[3] This rejection is accomplished in a most cavalier manner, no detailed consideration being undertaken; instead the theory is condemned on the sole grounds that the classification into types A and B is too precise and does not take account of several contrasting features within the types, e.g. the absence of an apse at Pompeii, of interior arcades at Trèves and the appearance of the square plan at Otricoli. All that needs to be said in reply is that a careful examination of Leroux's thesis in full indicates that he was well aware of the differences within the types, but regarded, correctly it would seem to me, these differences as of no primary significance and in no way affecting the general argument. Those scholars

[1] Leroux, *op. cit.*, pp. 139f., 150f., 215.

[2] e.g. R. Schultze, 'Basilika', *Römisch-Germanische Forschungen*, II, 1928; Cabrol-Leclerq, *Dictionnaire*, XII, 1936, cols. 2618–2622; Valentine Müller, 'The Roman Basilica', *A.J.A.*, XLI, 1937, pp. 250–1, this is an interesting elaboration of Leroux's theory, emphasizing the influence of Roman architecture upon the two basic types; cf. L. Bréhier, 'Les origines de la basilique chrétienne', *Bulletin Monumental*, LXXXVI, 1927, pp. 221–49.

[3] e.g. Lassus, *op. cit.*, p. 88; P. Lemerle, 'A propos des origines de l'édifice cultuel chrétien', *Bulletin de la Classe des Lettres et des Sciences Morales et Politiques*, XXXIV, 1948, p. 309.

who still withhold acceptance of the theory maintain a hope that further archaeological discoveries will provide the key; but, as already stated, this attitude arises from a failure to appreciate the nature of the problem which is not to find an immediate prototype—it would for example make little difference if a complete Christian basilica, with all the characteristic features, dating from before the Diocletian persecution, were brought to light—but to set the Christian basilica in the right line of architectural development. All that archaeological discoveries have revealed since 1913 is that there was a widespread tendency during the second and third centuries A.D. in all branches of architecture, funeral, imperial and religious, towards the adoption of an oblong building with interior colonnades.

The only serious rival to this solution at the present day is that which lays stress on the hypaethron. Although this has already been rejected above, further consideration of the antecedents of the hypaethron is desirable, since if it can be shown to belong to a line of development independent of that of the basilica, then its relationship with the basilica may be more precisely defined, at the same time as enabling its claim to be the model from which Christian architects drew their inspiration to be finally disallowed.

The megaron, from which the naos developed, was also the ancestor of the *stoa* or portico, which is in fact nothing else than an elongated megaron with one side wall replaced by a colonnade.[1] Examination of the literary usage of the term stoa indicates that on occasion it was regarded as synonymous with the word *basilike*, the two could be employed interchangeably. Basilike was also applied to buildings which consisted of an open court surrounded by covered colonnades; while basilikai could denote the colonnades themselves.[2] Here are all the main features of the basilike or the Kaisarion, erected by Julius Caesar at Antioch; this was an open court surrounded by porticos, preceding a vaulted apse

[1] Leroux, *op. cit.*, pp. 81, 184ff.

[2] Glanville Downey, 'The architectural significance of the use of the words *stoa* and *basilike* in classical literature', *A.J.A.*, XLI, 1937, pp. 194–211.

[32]

with a statue of the dictator.[1] It was in fact a hypaethral basilica which is quite evidently to be derived from the Greek stoa, since its main characteristic was the covered colonnade. The circular axis however must be attributed primarily to Egyptian influence which penetrated Greece about the third century B.C. Hence the hypaethron is not the prototype of the Christian basilica nor its descendent, the relationship between them is that they both derive independently from a common ancestor, the megaron. There is however one further point of contact, viz. the atrium, which was indeed nothing else than an open court surrounded by colonnades i.e. a hypaethron. A survival of the incipient Christian complex of basilica and atrium may possibly be seen in the building, surprisingly neglected by archaeologists, erected by Cassian *c*. A.D. 415 at Marseilles. This consists of a diminutive basilica, its nave only three metres wide, which opens on to a triple portico with circular axis as at Marusinac.[2] Since it was built at the entrance to the grotto where, according to tradition, St Victor was buried, this is another example of a funeral basilica, whatever the other uses, e.g. monastic, to which it was put; the small shrine has only to be enlarged in accordance with type B to produce the familiar Roman arrangement of church preceded by atrium.[3]

In view of the conclusion that the Christian basilica is a direct descendent of the megaron it is unnecessary to follow M. Leroux fully in his argument that it developed

[1] The similarity with the funeral basilica at Marusinac is to be noted.

[2] R. Busquet, *Histoire de Marseille*, 1945, pp. 53ff.

[3] It may be tentatively suggested, though there are certain obvious objections, that the term 'basilica' as applied to the main building may have been transferrred from the colonnaded hypaethron attached to it. Further light on this may be shed by the discovery of the Stoa Basileios at Athens. Excavations have been in progress for some years in the Athenian agora and a stoa has been brought to light on the west side and identified with the stoa of Zeus (H. A. Thompson, 'Buildings on the West Side of the Agora', *Hesperia*, VI, 1937, pp. 1–226). R. Martin ('La Stoa Basileios, Portiques à ailes et lieux d'assemblée', *Bulletin de Correspondance Hellénique*, LXVI–LXVII, 1942–3, pp. 274–98) argues that this is identical with the Stoa Basileios; J. Travlos, on the other hand (*Hesperia*, Supplement VIII, 1949, pp. 382–93), considers that they are distinct and the Stoa Basileios still awaits discovery. In view of this division of opinion no certain conclusions can be drawn at this stage of the excavations.

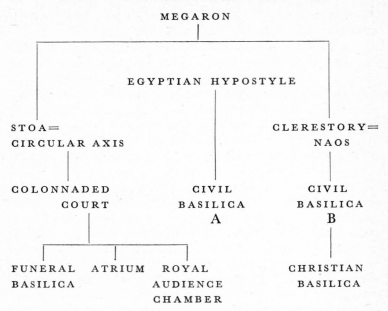

under the direct influence of certain buildings constructed by pagan bodies.[1] He instances two in particular: the Baccheion at Athens, on the western side of the Acropolis, which was the meeting place of the Iobacchoi, followers of Dionysius, dating from the second century A.D., and an edifice at Rome on the Janiculum of the third century, both of which present the basilica plan.[2] It is however scarcely credible that these small isolated examples could have exerted so immense an influence, rather their existence indicates that in the second and third centuries A.D. religious communities were adopting a similar type of building, and indeed it does not require an architectural genius to devise an oblong hall with two rows of columns to support the roof.

[1] For other theories, not here discussed since they scarcely merit serious consideration, *vide* H. Leclerq, *Manuel d'archéologie chrétienne*, I, 1907; R. Lemaire, *L'origine de la basilique latine*, 1911.

[2] To which may now be added the basilica of the Porta Maggiore, *Journal of Roman Studies*, IX, 1919, pp. 78ff.

Equally untenable is the eclectic theory[1] which sees the basilica as a combination of ideas from the private house with atrium or peristyle, from the *cellae memoriae* or funeral chapels with single or triple apse, from hypaethrons connected both with funeral and imperial architecture, and from the civil and private basilicas with their interior colonnades. There is no question that many and diverse influences bore upon early Christian art but the problem of the basilica's origin is reducible to this: either it already existed in pagan architecture or the Christians were the first to create it; only if the latter statement be correct is there any question of an amalgamation of different elements. But it has already been seen that the characteristics of the normal Christian basilica were contained in pagan edifices before the construction of the first churches and the eclectic theory is only of value in explaining those secondary elements, such as the atrium and transepts, which were not essential parts of the simple basilical type and plan.

A further question now arises. The Christian basilica is not only to be found in Rome but also in the East; was the type then created in the West and thence transported to the Hellenistic coastlands of Asia Minor and Syria, or did the reverse process take place?

When Constantine wrote to Macarius of Jerusalem about the projected Church of the Holy Sepulchre, he instructed the bishop to build the finest basilica yet seen,[2] but he did not consider it necessary to give any further details about it, thus intimating that the term βασιλική was well understood and had a definite connotation. This indeed is only to be expected, for the East was Christian before the West and in the provinces of Asia Minor especially there were flourishing communities before the Peace of the Church. In the Hellenized districts the basilica would appear to be indigenous and likewise in Italy it seems to have been created locally. This

---

[1] Tentatively revived at the present day by Lemerle, *op. cit.*, pp. 306–8; 'Aux origines de l'architecture chrétienne. Découvertes et théories nouvelles', *Revue Archéologique*, XXXIII, 1949, pp. 167–94.

[2] Eusebius, *Vita Const.*, iii. 34.

is not impossible, since both East and West, instead of the one directly influencing the other, could have derived their inspiration from a common model. Further when it is noted that the majority of the civil basilicas in Italy are to be found in those towns most subject to Greek influence, Copia, Thurmium and Pompeii, whence they probably spread to Rome, and when the general indebtedness of Western architecture to Greek ideas during the imperial era is taken into account, it is reasonable to suppose that the Christian basilica, derived as it was ultimately from the naos, came into being independently in both East and West at approximately the same date. The needs of worshipping communities in both parts of the civilized world being identical, nothing was more natural than that they should produce similar buildings, each emanating from a common prototype.

The general aspect of the basilica, modified by Christian usage, was that of a single room, its horizontal perspective being emphasized by parallel colonnades which seemed to converge on the altar standing close to one end on the middle axis. This was the focal point of the building and around it priesthood and laity gathered for the celebration of the liturgy, each section of the community having its prescribed place. In the centre of the semi-circular apse, roofed by a half dome, the bishop had his throne, the cathedra, on either side of which were the seats of the presbyters; hence the use of the term *presbyterium* for this part of the church. It was also variously known as the *exedra* or *concha* because of its shape; as the *bema* because it was raised by several steps above the main floor and as the *tribuna* or *tribunal* because it was similar to the platform occupied by the magistrates in the civil basilica. The superior clergy were separated from the rest of the congregation by the altar around which the deacons were grouped. It stood on the chord of the apse, usually above a *confessio* or repository for the relics of the saints and beneath a *ciborium* or baldachin. This in turn was fenced off by a balustrade or chancel of marble.

The great rectangular hall itself was divided by parallel

rows of columns into aisles of which there was always an odd number. The centre one, the nave, corresponded to the apse in width and was equivalent to the sum of the side aisles. The central height of the basilica was very much less than its total breadth and the height of each aisle, including the nave, was only a fraction greater than its width[1] so that the horizontal perspective was strongly accentuated. Here in the main body of the church, the inferior clergy, the choir, and the laity had their place. Men and women were carefully separated, but the method of separation differed from region to region. In Greek lands tribunes were provided over the side aisles for the women, but where these were absent the disposition could be either transverse, the men being across the nave and aisles at the front and behind them the women (as in North Syria, where there was a local predilection for doors in the south wall), or longitudinal, in which case the men were generally on the right and the women on the left. This latter arrangement seems to have been the more usual and the *Testamentum Domini*[2] assigns the southern aisle to the men and the northern to the women, thus apparently leaving the nave unoccupied; this is a Syrian document and it is now known that in many Syrian churches there was an exedra,[3] from which the bishop delivered his sermon, occupying a large portion of the nave. In Greece however a similar practice is to be observed; in Basilica A at Philippi the central nave is divided from the side aisles by a double *stylobate*, on the inner line of which there is a row of columns and on the outer a continuous chancel, thus rendering communication between the aisles and the nave impossible, except by openings at the extremities. Since the stone basement between the columns is smooth and well worn is was obviously utilised for seating[4] and so one may tentatively

[1] One-ninth to two-sevenths, *vide* Lowrie, *op. cit.*, p. 108.

[2] *Gerasa, City of the Decapolis*, ed. by C. H. Kraeling, 1938, p. 183.

[3] *vide postea*, p. 96.

[4] Other seats were at times provided, especially for the aged and infirm (*Const. Ap.*, II. 57) either wooden or stone benches (the βάθρα of Eusebius, *H.E.* x. 4, 44); traces of the latter have been found in Basilica B at Thebes, at Marusinac and elsewhere.

assign such groups as ascetics, virgins, widows and deacon-
esses to the sides of the nave along the colonnades, the
central space being left free for the deacons to circulate.[1]
The final division of the building was the porch in which
catechumens and penitents were allowed to stand.

It is not possible to continue this general description any
further, because churches of the basilica type, although
similar in their main architectural disposition, differ in
certain details by means of which they may be classified into
four groups: these are the Roman, the Hellenistic, the
Oriental and the Transverse.[2]

In the Roman or Latin basilica parallel rows of marble
columns, which were not fluted in order that the smooth
polished surface might reflect the rich colours of the mosaics
adorning the apse and the walls, supported long architraves[3]
on the abacus of each column, as in St Maria Maggiore. This
beam in turn bore the weight of the clerestory, on top of
which the timbered gable roof rested, a flat ceiling hiding the
tangle of rafters and thus maintaining the horizontal line
of the building at the same time as improving its acoustics.
The ceiling was divided by the beams into hollow spaces
which were covered with panels known as *lacunaria*.[4] None of
those in churches have been preserved intact but early
descriptions of them indicate that they were lavishly decorated with gold, and discoveries at Pompeii witness to the use
of geometrical designs in yellow, red and purple. The roof
itself was of wood, usually covered with terra cotta tiles, but
sometimes with lead or bronze.[5] The upper wall, rising
above the lean-to roofs of the side aisles, which were at the
same angle as the gable and of the same material, allowed
the daylight direct admission into the nave through windows

[1] P. Lemerle, *Philippes et la Macédoine orientale*, 1945, pp. 351, 357.

[2] This classification is only a general one; for differences within the groups see
especially the geographical distribution in Chap. VI.

[3] A few examples of the architrave in churches are found in Syria (Lassus,
op. cit., pp. 67, 68) where it seems to have been adopted to facilitate the construction of galleries; but its use was negligible.

[4] A style traditional to the Greek temple.

[5] St Peter's was covered with bronze tiles by Honorius I; *Lib. Pont. Vita Honor.*

which usually corresponded to the spaces between the columns. There were no windows in the apse nor in the side aisles, but the façade frequently had three as well as the gable of the transept. These openings were covered either with perforated slabs of marble and alabaster or with a metal latticework, the small apertures being usually left open thus providing a convenient means of ventilation, although sometimes they were filled with glass or translucent stone as in St Lorenzo, in which case the material used was colourless so that the tones of the mosaic should not be affected.

A noticeable feature of the Roman basilica was the transept,[1] which was developed by extending the chancels into the nave and across the aisles. Except in the Lateran basilica, it was usually narrower than the nave and it did not extend beyond the side walls, thus preserving the rectangular plan, although this rule was not always observed e.g. in St Peter's and St Paul's. The whole of the transept was raised like the floor of the apse above the level of the rest of the church and the altar was placed not immediately under the apsidal arch but on the line separating the transept from the nave.

The origin of the transept would appear to have been twofold; on the one hand to provide adequate accommodation both for the clergy between the altar and the apse and for the tables of the *prothesis*, in the wings, on which the faithful placed their gifts of bread and wine at the offertory in the Eucharist;[2] on the other hand to provide a large space around the tomb of the patron saint. The first of these may be termed a *transept-prothesis*, the second a *transept-martyrium*.[3] In Rome the transepts are all of one architectural type, viz.

[1] It can however be regarded no longer as a distinctive feature since recent excavations reveal that it was not unusual in the Hellenistic basilica, *vide postea*, p. 46.

[2] One table would no doubt have been sufficient, but the separation of the sexes probably involved the use of two, one in each of the wings. In churches where there was no transept, tables of the prothesis were placed at the extremities of the aisles, being screened either by chancels or curtains. The 'seven altars of purest silver, weighing each 200 lb.' which, according to the *Liber Pontificalis*, were given by Constantine to the Lateran, were probably tables of this kind, the number corresponding to the seven deacons of Rome.

[3] Lemerle, *op. cit.*, pp. 375–89.

they are formed by cutting short the aisles and colonnades at a greater or less distance from the eastern wall and leaving between the two a transverse rectangular space. The transept of the Lateran is a transept-prothesis, since no tomb is contained therein, while those of St Peter's and St Paul's are probably to be classified as transepts-martyria.[1]

The exterior appearance of the Roman basilica was in marked contrast to its interior, for the lavish decoration of the presbyterium and the nave had nothing in common with the undressed brick[2] of the outer walls and the bare projecting semidome of the apse. Since the edifice was often surrounded by other buildings its unprepossessing character was not very noticeable and some trouble was taken to render the more conspicuous façade as attractive as possible. There were two types of façade: the central gable, following the outline of the structure behind it, and the screen façade with square top which was usually made to overhang. The surface was at times broken up by a line of cuneiform bricks placed diagonally along the edge and the base of the gable, but in the more important churches, such as St Peter's, St Maria Maggiore and St John Lateran, a veneer of mosaic was applied from the summit to the portico. The portico itself, in which the penitents had their place, was either an independent arcade or one side of the quadrangular atrium. This was an open court, paved with marble, surrounded by a colonnade; it protected the church from the noise of the street, from which it was entered through a doorway, often overhung by a *propylon* or anteporch. This normally took the form of a single projecting arch supported on a pair of columns connected to the wall by architraves. In the centre of the atrium, like the impluvium in the private house, was the *phiale* or *cantharus*, a fountain used for ceremonial ablutions. Here under the covered porticos the catechumens came for

[1] The transepts of St Maria Maggiore and St Peter in vinculo are later additions.

[2] Until the Gothic wars, the bricks produced by the government factories were of excellent quality, the main change between the second and fifth centuries being a diminution in size; *vide* A. L. Frothingham, *The Monuments of Christian Rome*, 1908, p. 156.

instruction and the poor received their alms of bread; here too, when burial was permitted within the city limits, many of the faithful were laid to rest.

The flat-topped doors of the basilica were generally limited to the façade, there being one to each aisle; that of the nave was both the largest and the most richly decorated, Honorius I, for example, giving 975 pounds of silver for the ornamentation of the central doors of St Peter's. Particularly noteworthy are the carved cypress-wood doors of St Sabina at Rome, the panels of which depict scenes from the Old and New Testaments. Bronze doors, i.e. wood overlaid with thin plates of metal, were also in use, and classical examples were employed, as in the Lateran Baptistery, the doors of which came originally from the Baths of Caracalla and those of SS Cosmas and Damianus which incorporates the ancient temple of Romulus.

A typical example of this Latin basilica, which was confined almost exclusively to Rome itself, was the old St Peter's;[1] its foundation was laid shortly after A.D. 333, in part over an ancient pagan cemetery,[2] and until its destruction some 1,200 years later it was the finest Constantinian church that had been preserved (*Fig. 10*).

A flight of thirty five steps led up from the street to a propylon consisting of two columns, which now decorate the fountain of Paul V on the Janiculum, and bronze doors through which access was obtained to the atrium. This court, measuring 212 feet by 235, was surrounded by porticos for which over forty columns were employed, and in the centre was a magnificent fountain. The church was entered by five doors and was divided into the same number of aisles by eighty-eight columns and eight pilasters of various orders, taken from antique monuments, some of marble, some of granite. Two of those which were formerly near the door, of African marble, now flank the main entrance to the present

---

[1] The most ancient description of St Peter's is by Petrus Mallius, *Historia Basilicae antiquae S. Petri* in the *Codex Vat.*, 3627.

[2] W. Seston, 'Hypothèse sur la date de la basilique constantinienne de Saint-Pierre de Rome', in *Cahiers Archéologiques*, II, 1947, pp. 153–9.

portico. The columns of the main nave, which was eighty feet across, supported architraves above which the clerestory wall was pierced by arched windows, the daylight showing the bare rafters of the roof. At the end of the nave, the triumphal arch was decorated with a mosaic, depicting the

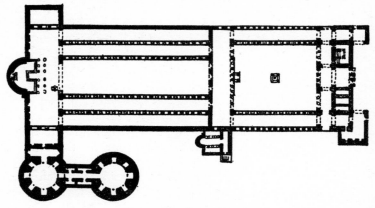

Fig. 10. St Peter, Rome.

Emperor presented to Christ by Peter and offering Him a model of the church. Beneath was the inscription:

Quod duce te mundus surrexit ad astra triumphans
Hanc Constantinus victor tibi condidit aulam.[1]

Another mosaic of Christ and the two Apostles Peter and Paul adorned the semicircular projecting apse, in the centre of which was the cathedra flanked by the seats of the presbyters. Before the tribune the church opened out into a transept which extended beyond the aisles. Here stood the altar, the focus of the whole building, above the confessio, where the remains of the patron saint were preserved.

The second of the four groups into which the basilica may be classified is the Hellenistic, which was by far the most popular. Although it extended westwards to the shores of the Adriatic, reaching Parenzo and Ravenna, it was mainly

[1] M. A. R. Tuker and Hope Malleson, *Handbook to Christian and Ecclesiastical Rome*, 1, 1900, p. 60.

III. Basilica at Ruwêhā, from the southwest

IV.   Interior of Basilica at Ruwêhā, from the northwest

confined to the Eastern Mediterranean. It was to be found all along the coastline and it passed from thence inland by the routes giving the Greeks easy access to the interior, advancing from Antioch into Central Syria and beyond, from Alexandria up the valley of the Nile, and along the North African coast into Numidia and Mauretania. In southern Asia Minor it moved eastwards as far as the chain of the Taurus.

The main components of the Hellenistic basilica were identical with those of the Roman, both being derived from the same prototype, and there is therefore no need to repeat their description here. There was the same division of the church into nave, aisles and apse, the same use of chancels, and the same disposition of the several orders of the community, except for the women who were relegated to a gallery (*matroneum*) built over the side aisles.[1] There were however certain marked differences, in particular the use of archivolts and the incorporation of the vestibule into the rectangular structure to form a *narthex* (*Fig. 11*).

Fig. 11. St Apollinare Nuovo, Ravenna.

Excellent though the architrave was for emphasising the horizontal perspective of the building, it had two defects: first, it provided a poor support for the wall above it and second, it tended to disrupt the unification of the room of the congregation by isolating the side aisles. To remedy this

[1] The galleries of such Roman churches as St Lorenzo and St Agnese are later and due to Byzantine influence: they are rare in North Africa, Palestine and Syria, but frequent along the littoral of Asia Minor, at Constantinople and throughout Greece.

E   [43]

archivolts were introduced, i.e. arches springing from the columns[1] which could now be placed at wider intervals thus allowing a freer prospect from the aisles. Despite this alteration, the horizontal principle was preserved by the use of a cornice or a frieze and by the design of the mosaics, such as the procession of saints advancing towards the enthroned Christ, in St Apollinare Nuovo at Ravenna. There was however a limit to the weight the columns could bear, if they had been placed too far apart the result would have been dislocation, so in order to increase further the space between the supports it was necessary to substitute pillars for the columns, since these, having a more solid base, permitted the construction of a broader arch. In the Early Christian period the pillar was not often used except in central Syria where the absence of pagan buildings from which columns could be obtained and the heavy weight of the structure which was exclusively of stone, due to the lack of wood, rendered it a common feature of the Hauran basilicas. These stone-roofed churches were divided into central and side aisles by two rows of low square piers which supported arches spanning the nave, as well as longitudinal arches and two transverse arches one above the other, of which the lower spanned the side aisle and the upper the gallery above it; they were consequently cruciform in cross-section as at Resâfah. In the West pillars were not uncommon, particularly in North Africa, e.g. at Orléansville, but in Italy there are only three churches in which they are known to have been used, St Sinforosa, the basilica attached to the Xenodochium at Porto, and the older basilica of St Felix at Nola which St Paulinus replaced by one with columns. However, pillars were always employed to carry the triumphal arch which spanned the entrance to the apse and with the development of dome architecture they became the chief supports, the

[1] The archivolt would appear to have passed from Iran and Mesopotamia to Antioch in the third century, whence it spread to the Syrian hinterland during the next hundred years, shortly before it was adopted throughout the Mediterranean area, where the earliest example is probably in the palace of Diocletian at Spalato. J. Lassus, *op. cit.*, pp. 71–96; J. Strzygowski, *L'ancien art chrétien de Syrie*, 1936, p 185.

column being relegated to the position of a mere decorative adjunct.

The Hellenistic basilica, like its Latin counterpart, was usually preceded by an atrium, although, particularly in Syria, there are exceptions to this. Occasionally the church was surrounded by a rectangular wall, the enclosed space corresponding to the *temenos* in which the Greek temple stood. At il-Anderîn, the great wall around the South church was used for *arcosolia*; the 'Bizzos' church at Ruwêhā was also similarly enclosed, but the tombs in this instance were placed inside the court in two great monumental structures. The Hellenistic and the Roman atrium were not entirely identical, for whereas the portico along one side of the latter served as the vestibule to the church, this was incorporated into the Hellenistic basilica to form an integral part of the building.[1] Thus in the West, the vestibule was open to the outside, while in the East, the narthex, as it was called, was closed to the outside by a door but open into the church. In Syria large porches were included in the main structure and the many different façades are striking in their originality; the general scheme comprised a flight of steps leading up into the narthex which was surmounted by an open loggia, flanked by two towers balancing the central gable of the nave.[2] The doors of this entrance were richly ornamented, sometimes being of carved wood, sometimes of incised or relief stone. There was a greater use of windows, as they were introduced not only into the clerestory and the gable but also in the walls of the aisles, as at Ravenna. In the sixth century the apse too, which was polygonal externally, was pierced with windows, apparently because of the symbolic interest

[1] The interior narthex does not appear either in Rome or Palestine in the Constantinian buildings, nor in Syria, where there are porches rather than narthexes; it was however a constant feature of the early Christian basilicas in Greece and in the Hellenistic coastlands of the Aegean. In the sixth century it became habitual in the Hellenistic basilica, being diffused under the influence of Justinian's architecture, thus e.g. at Bethlehem the Constantinian basilica which had no narthex was reconstructed and one added. The narthex may possibly derive from the *chalcidicum* of the civil basilicas.

[2] e.g. basilica at Turmanin; Lowrie, *op. cit.*, Fig. 32.

attached to the rising sun shining on the Eucharistic elements; but this innovation, allowing the ingress of brilliant shafts of light, tended to spoil the effect of the mosaics.

The roof was covered with lead and bronze, as in the West; the Church of the Apostles at Constantinople having gilt tiles so that the sunlight all but blinded the spectator.[1] At Ravenna coloured glazed tiles were used, being arranged to form geometrical patterns. Ornate ceilings were also in vogue, although in Syria the presence of windows high in the gable indicates that the rafters were there left visible.

It was customary in the past to assert with confidence that the transept was not found in the Hellenistic basilica,[2] but now eight examples are known in Greece[3] all dating from the later fourth and the fifth centuries and there are many in Asia Minor, e.g. at Corycus, Sagalossos and Perga. The transept however is not found in Syria, only one example is so far known in Palestine—the Church of the Multiplication of the Loaves—a further single example is to be found in Egypt—the basilica of St Arcadius at St Menas, while in North Africa there are no traces. From this it is reasonable to suppose that the transept in the East, like the narthex, was originally the creation of Greece, and it is to be found in profusion only in those districts where Hellenistic influences were predominant. Five of the eight examples in Greece conform to the Roman type, i.e. the transept is obtained by cutting short the aisles and colonnades and leaving open a rectangle perpendicular to the nave; but a second type is presented by the three remaining basilicas, viz. the side aisles and colonnades bend outwards at right-angles, near the east end, without being interrupted, and then turn through another right angle to join the east wall, thus leaving a free space in the centre, e.g. basilica A at Philippi. This type is doubtless a Greek creation and was devised in order to accommodate the rite of the prothesis.[4] In the West, as noted

---

[1] Eus., *Vita Const.*, iv. 58. [2] e.g. Lowrie, *op. cit.*, p. 126.

[3] Lemerle, *op. cit.*, p. 381.

[4] G. Soteriou, Ἡ πρόθεσις καὶ τὸ διακονικὸν ἐν τῇ ἀρχαίᾳ ἐκκλησίᾳ, Θεολογία, περίοδ. Β', τόμ. Α.' Athens, 1941, pp. 76–100.

above, at the Eucharist the faithful brought up their gifts at
the offertory to the tables of prothesis, but in the East the
gifts were handed over to the deacon before the service,
probably in the *diakonikon* or vestry, some of the bread and
wine being then placed on the tables of prothesis by the
deacons and carried up by them alone at the offertory.[1]
These transepts would then be used as *pastophoria*,[2] i.e. places
for the setting aside of the bread and wine prior to the
Eucharist.

A second architectural expedient to provide for this rite
was the tripartite sanctuary i.e. the construction of two
symmetrical side chambers flanking the apse and opening
into the side aisles. Frequently this tripartite sanctuary was
enclosed by a single eastern wall (*Fig. 12*) and it seems evident

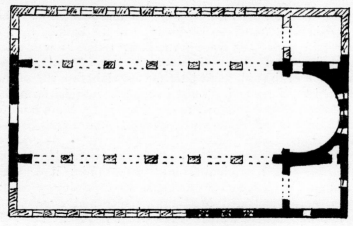

Fig. 12. The East church, Zebed.

that this plan was adopted originally in the fourth century
for aesthetic reasons in order to preserve the rectangular
shape of the building on the exterior.[3] In the early fifth

[1] Dix, *op. cit.*, pp. 110–23.   [2] *Const. Ap.*, II, 57.

[3] H. C. Butler, 'The Tychaion of Es-Sanamein and the plan of early churches
in Syria,' *Revue Archéologique*, 1906, II, pp. 413ff., considers that the tripartite
sanctuary derived from pagan prototypes, but the examples adduced are from
southern Syria while the form first appeared in North Syria.

century in North Syria the two side chambers ceased to be symmetrical, one of them continued as a closed room communicating with the aisle by a small door and with the apse by an even smaller one, the other was given an arch which spanned the width of the aisle in the same way as the triumphal arch spanned the nave. It is usual to assert that this last chamber was the prothesis, where priest and deacon performed the preparation and the preliminary oblation before the litany,[1] while the second was the diakonikon. Re-examination of many of those churches with this disposition has however led Lassus to a different conclusion, and he has assembled evidence which certainly proves that the common theory is based on an anachronism and that the chamber with the arch was in fact a *martyrium*, i.e. a chapel where the relics of the martyr were enshrined; the archaeological data allows him to point to the year 420 as the approximate date when this invasion of the basilica by the cult of the saints took place in the East.[2] Later, however, the convenience of these chambers for the pre-Eucharist collection of the gifts (and later for the elaborate rite of the prothesis) was recognized, and in the symmetrical form the tripartite sanctuary spread to the littoral and hinterland of Asia Minor in the fifth century, finally penetrating to Greece in the sixth century.

The oriental basilica, also known as the barn church and the *Hallenkirche*, originated in Mesopotamia; it secured a temporary footing in Armenia and passing through Anatolia it penetrated to Cyprus, Crete and Greece. Its most distinguishing feature was a blind nave, i.e. the wall of the nave was not carried up above the aisles. Its ground plan was similar to that of the Roman and Hellenistic groups, but it was shorter in length in order to compensate for

---

[1] A distinction must be noted here between the preliminary collection of the gifts and that which developed from it viz. the elaborate rite of the prothesis, an introductory service performed before the Eucharist proper. The anachronism referred to in the text is in supposing that the elaborate rite, requiring a special chamber, was sufficiently popular at this date to exercise so widespread an influence on architecture.

[2] *op. cit.*, pp. 162–83, and *vide postea*, p. 88.

the lack of a clerestory, light being obtained through the windows in the apse and in the side walls. The roof was not timbered but invariably vaulted, a feature which is of Asiatic origin, being found in Persia, Mesopotamia and Syria. These vaults were supported on piers, sometimes with pillars as an adjunct. There was no atrium but a narthex was attached to the building, consisting in central Anatolia of an entrance chamber of columns and arches communicating with the nave by a door. Two other chambers were laid against this, one on either side; that to the north being accessible by means of an arch, while that to the south could only be entered by a door leading out of the aisle inside the church (*Fig. 13*).

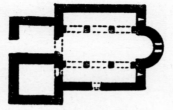

Fig. 13. Maden Dagh.

The transverse basilica, as its name signifies, was a single nave at right angles to the line connecting the entrance door with the apse. This was a primitive Mesopotamian type to be found in the Tūr Abdīn, north east of Nisibis, in Armenia, in Cappadocia and in the Hauran (*Fig. 14*). In Eastern Syria a more complex edition of the same plan, emanating probably from Arabia, was achieved by combining a series of arched units consisting of a line of rib arches supported on piers, the surrounding walls being carried up to the level of the crown of the arches which were then roofed with stone slabs. This type had no influence on the further development of Christian art, unless it be in the formation of the transept, but this remains only a conjecture as sufficient evidence is not forthcoming.

The basilica, in one form or another, had an area of distribution ranging from Mesopotamia and Syria to Great

Britain; in the West it was perpetuated for over a thousand years, but in the East it ceased to be in general use after the fifth century when it was ousted by churches of the central type.

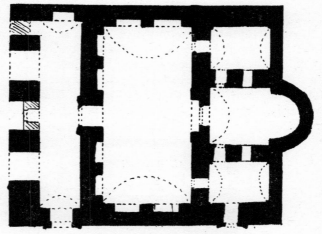

Fig. 14. Mar Yakub, Salah.

NOTE

A type of basilica, which has not been listed in the above classification because it is confined to North Africa, is that having an apse at both ends. There are in Tunisia at least six or seven churches in which this disposition is to be found, and in Algeria at least three. In the latter area these secondary apses were certainly used for burial, but in Tunisia only three have traces of sarcophagi or relics, while that at Henchir Goraat es-Zid probably contained a font.

III

THE CENTRAL TYPE OF ARCHITECTURE

B Y THE CENTRAL type of architecture no one uniform plan is indicated but the general principle of eurhythmic disposition around a central vertical axis. The buildings to which this classification applies did not develop from the basilica, they existed by the side and independent of it from the beginning of Christian architecture. They were employed at first by the Church solely as memorial edifices to enclose the tomb of a saint or to mark a place hallowed by association with our Lord.

In the West and particularly in Italy few of these martyria were erected; the addition of the transepts to the basilica, thus producing the symbolic cruciform plan, and the placing of the altar in direct communication with the sacred relics allowed the Eucharist and the cult of the saints to develop in unity. In the East on the other hand these two developed independently, each with its own ceremonies and each with its own peculiar type of architecture: the centralized martyria for the saints and the rectangular basilica for the Eucharist. When the translation of relics, in the latter half of the fifth century, allowed the cult of martyrs to leave the cemeteries, the practice arose of dedicating each and every church in honour of an individual saint whose name it adopted and whose remains it henceforth enshrined. The buildings erected under this influence naturally perpetuated the traditional form of a *martyrium extra muros*, with its centralized plan and its resemblance to a tomb, but as the edifice was also to be used for the regular celebration of the liturgy which demanded not a vertical axis but a horizontal perspective, the architects were faced with the problem of modifying the primitive form in order to combine it with the basilica; hence arose the centralized churches as distinct from the centralized martyria, from which however they had originated.[1]

One of the characteristic features of the central type of architecture, although one that is not invariable, is the dome, which itself is of great antiquity, there being evidence of its existence in Egypt at the beginning of the dynastic period[2] and in Chaldea and Assyria from an early date.[3] It was first used in conjunction with a round building, the rotunda resting directly on the outside wall. Such was the Pantheon at Rome, one of the most remarkable examples of this type, its height being over 148 feet, while the interior diameter was 142 feet. The immense weight of the brick dome was carried on a wall of mass concrete 20 feet thick, which was broken by a series of eight niches, alternately square and semi-circular, in front of which rows of columns were placed for decorative effect. The entrance was through a vast portico 104 feet wide, with columns 47 feet high. Buildings of this kind were constructed by the Romans as baths and mausolea, and in the East similar edifices were to be found, the most note-worthy being the Marneion at Gaza and the Serapeion at Alexandria. It was originally believed that this plan was a Roman invention, but recent discoveries at Pergamum and Constantinople suggest that it may have been the creation of the Hellenistic mind under strong oriental influence, since its use in Greek architecture is confined to a small group of deities, e.g. Dionysus and Aphrodite, all of whom were affected by alien Asiatic cults.

This plan was adopted by the Church for some of its memorial buildings, amongst the earliest examples being the two small rotundas which adjoined the old St Peter's. They

[1] A. Grabar, *Martyrium, Recherches sur le culte des reliques religieux et l'art chrétien antique*, 1946, I, cap. ii; Lassus, *op. cit.*, pp. 112–60.

[2] K. A. C. Creswell, *Early Muslim Architecture*, 1932, I, p. 304.

[3] A dome is represented on a bas-relief from the palace of Sennacherib, 705–681 B.C.

were both adorned with eight niches and one of them, which was dedicated to St Petronilla in the eighth century, originally belonged to the family of Theodosius and the other, dedicated to St Andrew, was probably also intended for a mausoleum when constructed. The tomb of Theodoric at Ravenna, another circular building, bears traces of Syrian influence; it consists of two rooms, the lower being in the form of a cross, the upper being round; externally it is a decagon, surmounted by a colossal monolith of ashlar.

The obvious way to modify this plan in the interests of the Eucharist is exemplified by the church of St George at Salonika. Originally constructed at the end of the third century A.D., it was converted to Christian use and dedicated in honour of the saint in the fifth century, when an ambulatory (now destroyed) was built around it and a choir with an apse was added at the east end (*Fig. 15*).

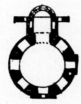

Fig. 15. St George, Salonika.

This simple plan was soon elaborated, the dome being carried on an inner rotunda of columns which was enclosed in an outer circular wall. One of these monuments, again memorial in intention, was erected by Constantine at Rome to enshrine the huge sarcophagus of porphyry in which the remains of his sister were placed. The cupola of St Costanza (324–6) is supported by twelve arcades resting on twelve coupled shafts and its thrust is partly received by the walls and vaults of the ambulatory. The thick outer wall of the ring-vault is recessed with apsidal niches in groups of three between the two doors and the two larger apses. Entrance was made through a closed vestibule of oblong form with a hemicycle at each end, and the whole building was originally surrounded by a circular colonnade (*Fig. 16*). In the year following the completion of St Costanza work was begun on the Anastasis at Jerusalem. This too was a circular building which was erected over the Holy Sepulchre and covered with a wooden roof, part of the inner circle being left open to the sky. The plan of St Stephano Rotundo is essentially the same as that of St Costanza—its roof however, like that of the Anastasis, was of wood. The central drum is supported on

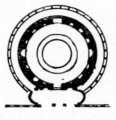

Fig. 16. St Costanza, Rome.

twenty columns and enclosed in a further twenty-eight columns which are intersected by four colonnaded wings. According to De Rossi[1] it was a Christian edifice of the fifth century, dedicated by Simplicius (468–82) and completed by John I (523–6); if this theory be accepted then the building is nothing less than exceptional, for there are no other examples of churches erected specifically for congregational use without adequate space being provided at the east end for a sanctuary; accordingly one is tempted to agree with those critics who consider it to be a transformed pagan building which may have been a temple of Faunus or Bacchus, or even the meat market of Nero. One further elaboration demands notice before passing on to the composite plan, viz. that according to which the circle was inscribed in an octagon which was enclosed in a second similarly placed octagon. This scheme was reproduced in the Mosque of Omar, erected in the years 688–91 upon Mount Moriah, on the site of the Jewish temple. Although it was founded by an Arab caliph to preserve the rock from which

[1] *Studi e Documenti di Storia e Diritto*, a. vii, 1886.

Mohammed began his flight through the heavens—the memorial intention is again evident—it was directly inspired by the work of the Constantinian artists, and there is no doubt that those responsible for its creation were themselves Byzantine. It is probable that the roof was at first open in the centre, like the church of the Ascension which in purpose it closely resembled, but it was provided later with a wooden dome (*Fig. 17*).[1]

Fig. 17. Mosque of Omar, Jerusalem.

This type of centralized building was incapable of further development, but to desert it was to be immediately faced with the problem of how to unite the circular dome with any other shape of support. At first the attempt was made to employ an octagonal base and, since the interior angles of this figure leave a relatively small gap to be bridged, the task was not over difficult. The first of the two solutions of which the architects availed themselves involved laying a slab across each angle thus doubling the number of the sides of the polygon; this process was then repeated—further slabs being introduced into each layer of masonry, until the angles were so depressed that an almost circular course was obtained on which the dome could finally be placed. The second expedient was the squinch, which consisted of a small arch or series of superimposed arches flung across each angle. It was an oriental discovery[2] and occurs in the palaces of Serbistan and Firouzabad, monuments of the Sassanian architecture of southern Persia, which date from the third to the fifth centuries A.D.

[1] K. A. C. Creswell, 'The Origin of the Plan of the Dome of the Rock', *British School of Archaeology in Jerusalem, Supplementary Papers* 2, 1924.
[2] cf. G. Millet, 'L'Asie Mineure', in *Revue Archéologique*, I, 1905, pp. 101–5.

The dome surmounting an octagon was a popular form for baptisteries and one of the earliest examples, erected by Constantine, San Giovanni in Fonte at Rome, comprises an octagon within an octagon. The central figure is constructed of eight immense porphyry columns on which rests an architrave, this in turn carries eight smaller columns supporting the drum of the lantern. The same plan was adopted by the architects of Constantine for the churches of the Holy Apostles at Constantinople and of the Nativity at Bethlehem, although in both these instances the buildings were commemorative, and rectangular basilicas were added for the celebration of the liturgy. At a later date the octagonal plan was taken into congregational use; such was the church of the Theotokos at Gerizim, built by the Emperor Zeno after

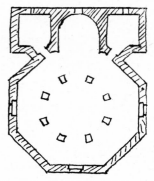

Fig. 18. Church of Mir'âyeh.

the Samaritan rising of 484, but here an eastern apse has been added. Standing free in the midst of a rectangular precinct, its roof is carried on an octagonal ring composed of eight piers and fourteen columns, two columns being placed between each pier except in front of the chancel. At the other three principal points of the compass there are doors in the octagonal outer wall approached by perrons. Unique among the buildings in which this plan is to be traced is the sixth-century church at Mir'âyeh in north-eastern Syria, which in effect comprises an octagon to which the east end of an ordinary basilica has been added. One side of the octagon is occupied by the triumphal arch, which is flanked by two side chambers reached by oblique passages just beside the apse. The interior is heaped high with debris and earth but it seems likely that there was originally a dome of mud-brick carried on an interior octagon of piers and arches (*Fig. 18*). The architect of another sixth-century building, the chapel at

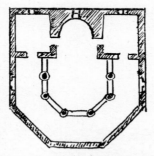

Fig. 19. Church of Midjleyyā.

Midjleyyā, has carried the fusion of basilica and martyrium even further, by sacrificing the rotunda. The east end of the octagon has been replaced by an apse and two sacristies which are contained by the three sides of a rectangle formed by the east wall and the prolongation eastwards of the north and south sides (*Fig. 19*).

The enclosure of two concentric similar octagons in a square was accomplished at Zor'ah in the church of St George (A.D. 515) (*Fig. 20*). Its outline has the form of a rectangle at the east end of which a space, equal to the difference between the rectangle and the square of its shorter side, is set off for two side chambers with a bema between them. From the bema opens a semicircular apse, polygonal at the exterior. Within the square to the west of the sanctuary an octagon was created by cutting off the interior angles, into which semicircular niches were introduced and within this great octagon a smaller one was made of eight angle piers carrying arches. The masonry in the spandrels immediately begins to warp forward, so that by the time it has been brought up to the level of the crowns of the arches the angles have been almost eliminated; a drum, circular within and octagonal without, pierced with windows just above the stone roof of the aisle, bears the tall sugar-loaf dome; the

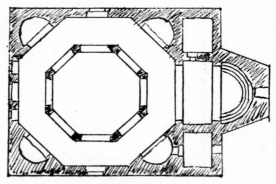

Fig. 20. St George, Zo'rah.

passage from octagon to circle was thus made by imperceptible degrees in the building up of the stone work.

Finally, there is the octagon contained within two squares of which the great sixth-century baptistery at Kal'at Sim'ân in northern Syria is an excellent example. The core of the building is an octagon within a square, the solid angles between the two figures being filled with both semicircular and square niches; in its east side there is an apse fashioned out of the projecting mass of masonry. The inner square is surrounded by a greater one which provides arched passages around the baptistery. The drum is roofed with an eight-sided pyramid of wood and the ambulatory by steep-pitched wooden lean-tos.

One of the most beautiful churches of the centralized type is that of St Vitale at Ravenna, which was erected during the reign of Justinian, the foundations being laid about 526 and the work being completed in 547. It consists of two concentric octagons with the bema and the apse extending beyond the

[58]

V.   Squinch, S. Clement, Angora, Asia Minor

VI. S. Vitale, Ravenna, with tomb of Galla Placidia in the foreground

perimeter on the eastern side. The eight great pillars of the central room support an octagonal drum to which the dome is joined by means of squinches. The ambulatory is divided into upper and lower galleries (both of them vaulted) which are intersected by seven niches. These niches are surmounted by half domes, each of which rests upon two columns so that there is a free prospect from the corridors into the central space (*Fig. 21*).

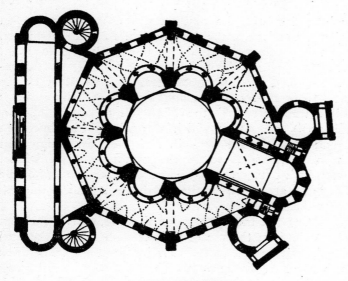

Fig. 21. St Vitale, Ravenna.

The origin of this plan and in particular the combination of the exedrae with the octagon has been the subject of much debate; the great Austrian scholar Strzygowski considering it to be a development of the niche-buttressed square, and other critics maintaining that it has evolved from the use of deep niches in a thick wall which was a constantly recurring feature of Roman construction.

According to Strzygowski, there are two principal forms of the square plan with niche abutment. First, the niche-buttressed square, showing the four buttresses projecting from the walls which stand free as a visible rectangle. Of this type he distinguishes three subdivisions: (a) the niche-buttressed square with buttresses on the axes only. This has a wide distribution not only in Armenia but also in north Mesopotamia and Georgia, the simplest surviving example being the church of Mastara in Armenia, c. A.D. 650; (b) the niche-buttressed square with both axial and diagonal buttresses; the church of Awan (c. 570) in Armenia and of Mzchet in Georgia (c. 600) are of this type; (c) domed churches without niche abutment, the dome resting on interior supports, e.g. the cathedral of Bagaran, Armenia, 624–31. The second principal form of the square plan is that according to which the buildings are composed of niche-buttresses only, the buttresses meeting each other at the corners without any intervening wall space. This series is divisible into three: (i) the quatrefoil consisting of four niches[1]; (ii) the sexfoil which was widely distributed in Georgia; and (iii) the octofoil. It is this last design that Strzygowski considers to be the prototype of St Vitale, Constantine's octagon which was erected on the site of the earlier baths at Antioch in the fourth century being the link between Armenia and Ravenna.[2]

The alternative theory, mentioned above, derives the plan of St Vitale from the use of recesses to break up the wall surface in many of the early centralized buildings. The thick outer wall of St Costanza is divided into quarters by two doors and two large apses; these spaces are decorated with groups of three niches which fulfil no functional purpose whatever, being merely a decorative motif. The same use of niches is to be noticed in many of the churches already described; thus there are seven rectangular recesses in St George at Salonika; and the church of St George at Zor'ah has apsidal niches and also the baptistery at Ḳal'at Sim'ân.

---

[1] cf. the martyrium excavated at Seleucia Pieria, *Antioch-on-the-Orontes*, III, *The Excavations, 1937–39*, 1941, pp. 35–54.

[2] J. Strzygowski, *The Origin of Christian Church Art*, 1923, pp. 57–67, cf. also the cathedral at Bosra which consists of a quatrefoil enclosed in a rectangle with a sanctuary added at the east end.

These niches had only to be opened clear through the walls for the inner room to be put into direct communication with the surrounding corridor. This was already effected in the *nymphaeum* in the Licinian Gardens, the so-called temple of Minerva Medica at Rome (A.D. 263–8) where ten niches open into the circular ambulatory.

Where the wall was comparatively thin, not admitting of deep niches between its two surfaces, if this traditional form of decoration was to continue in use it could only be accomplished by the construction of apsidal additions projecting beyond the walls. This is what has happened in the two baptisteries at Ravenna; four semicircular niches are added to each interior octagon, thus transforming the Orthodox Baptistery (*c.* 450) into the form of a square at the exterior, while the Arian Baptistery (early sixth century) suggests the shape of a cross. Eight false arches resting upon engaged columns preserve the harmony of the interior and the octagonal wall is carried up above the summit of the niches to provide a base for the dome. It is argued that a combination of these expedients, viz., the piercing of the niches and the construction of apsidal additions, would produce the central figure in the plan of St Vitale.

To decide between these two theories is by no means simple, since, whereas there are many dated monuments which seem to favour the second, their preservation is due entirely to chance, and there may have been many more buildings, either totally destroyed or still awaiting excavation, which would weigh the scales in the other direction. The crux of the problem lies in whether the niches in St Vitale are primarily decorative or functional. The dome is quite light, being constructed of terra-cotta pipes fitted into each other to form a spiral—a method which considerably diminishes the weight. The arched window openings in the drum serve to concentrate the weight upon the pillars, which are supported by radial walls extending to the perimeter where further pillars take the thrust. These radial walls, which are pierced above and below by arches to permit free circulation around the galleries, are quite adequate to preserve the

[61]

stability of the building. The niches therefore, while helping to distribute the weight and increase the torsional rigidity, are by no means essential, and if they were omitted the general equilibrium would be scarcely impaired. Comparison with the cathedral of Aachen substantiates this conclusion. The cathedral, which was connected with one of Charlemagne's palaces and consecrated in 805, was built under the direct influence of St Vitale, but the niches and the columns on the ground floor have been suppressed to re-establish a straightforward division between central octagon and ambulatory. The result is not so graceful as St Vitale, but it demonstrates quite clearly that the niches served no important functional purpose and that they are therefore primarily ornamental.[1] One may tentatively suggest that they were devised by an architect of genius, possibly of Syrian origin, influenced by Roman examples, who perceived their decorative possibilities as well as the slight addition they would make to the stability of the edifice as a whole.[2]

These considerations equally apply to the church of SS. Sergius and Bacchus at Constantinople, which was built at the same time. According to tradition it was erected by Justinian as a thankoffering to the two saints who had secured his reprieve, when under sentence of death, by appearing to the Emperor Anastasius. In plan it is an irregular square with a narthex at the west end and an apse at the east. The central octagon is composed of eight piers supporting a dome on squinches; the dome is made of sixteen compartments alternately flat and concave. Between the piers, pairs of columns are set in two tiers forming exedrae similar to those in St Vitale, except that the niche opposite the apse and the central niches on each side of this line were suppressed by carrying the line of columns straight across from pillar to pillar. The weight and thrust of the dome is taken by the piers which are linked across the surrounding corridor to the outside wall, and also by small buttresses

[1] N. Pevsner, *An Outline of European Architecture*, 1942, p. 18.

[2] J. B. Ward-Perkins, 'The Italian Element in Late Roman, and Early Mediaeval Architecture', *Proceedings of the British Academy*, 1947, pp. 163–94.

which pierce the roof of the ambulatory and are engaged with the sides of the drum. Its affinities both with St Vitale and with the Eastern octagonal type as at Zor'ah are sufficiently obvious to render further comment unnecessary (*Fig. 22*).

In seeking to combine the cupola with an octagonal basis the early Christian architects were faced with a problem whose solution was not hard to discover, since the eight-

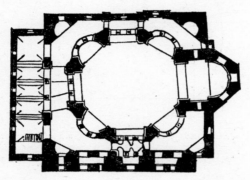

Fig. 22. SS Sergius and Bacchus, Constantinople.

sided figure already approximated to the circle of the dome. But the attempt to place a dome over a square was much more difficult and the means subsequently devised was correspondingly all the more brilliant. At first the two methods described above were employed, viz. the squinch, of which the earliest example in the West is in the fifth-century Baptistery of Soter at Naples, and the placing of slabs across the angles as in the Kalybé at Umm iz-Zētûn where the square is made into an octagon and the octagon into a thirty-two-sided polygon until finally an almost circular course is obtained on which the dome may rest. The third and most important expedient adopted to effect the transition from the square to the circle was the pendentive. The pendentive is a spherical triangle filling the spandrels of the arches supporting the dome; its base curves upwards and forwards until its angles meet those of its two neighbours on either side at the crowns of the adjoining arches. At an early stage in the development pendentive and dome formed one continuous whole, i.e. a domical vault, but later the pendentive became an independent entity, its circular upper

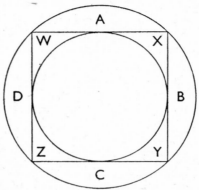

Remove *ABCD* and *WXYZ* are spherical triangular pendentives.

surface joining a horizontal ring of masonry on which the dome was placed.

The origin of this architectural device is shrouded in obscurity and amongst the many theories that have been advanced there are four which deserve special notice. The older and more conservative critics maintain that the pendentive was created in the West, basing their assertion on some few doubtful examples. Thus attention is drawn to the so-called pendentive on the Palatine Hill in the house of Augustus which was rebuilt by Domitian; to the continuous pendentives in the tomb called the Sedia del Diavolo and in the Casale dei Pazzi, both near the Via Nomentana and dating from the late second century A.D.[1] But these are rather to be classed as corbels and their horizontal section is almost flat while their inner surfaces are inclined planes.[2] A satisfactory pendentive was in fact unknown to the Romans and all the examples of the use of the dome in the West are either on circular buildings or over minute squares by means

[1] *vide* G. T. Rivoira, *Lombardic Architecture*, 1910, I.
[2] cf. J. A. Hamilton, *Byzantine Architecture and Decoration*, 1933, pp. 19—20.

of makeshift supports which could only be trusted on a small scale. Consequently, Strzygowski has turned to the East and affirms that the dome over a square is of purely Iranian origin. According to him the archetype of the domed building was the primitive wooden house of central Asia which consisted of a square room covered by a roof constructed by continuous corbelling. After the Aryan immigration into Iran, where wood was scarce, the plan was reproduced in sun-dried brick, the corner beams being replaced by brick arches or squinches. Passing into Armenia it was there translated into stone and with the introduction of the quatrefoil and the piercing of the solid walls with arches the spherical pendentive made its appearance. Thus the Armenian Christians of the fourth century are declared to have been the first to use a square building with a single dome as a church. The royal Arcasid tombs of Pre-Christian Armenia are also referred to as having exerted an influence, for these edifices are supposed to have been free-standing squares covered with a dome, like the square baptistery of A.D. 359 in the Church of St James at Nisibis.

Against this theory it must be recognized that nothing is known of the primitive wooden constructions of central Asia nor of the early sun-dried brick buildings of the Altai-Iran, and that so far no Armenian churches of the fourth century have been brought to light. Those Armenian monuments which have been discovered belong to the fifth and sixth centuries and many of these are vaulted basilicas without domes, while domed buildings of a much earlier date may still be seen in Syria, Mesopotamia and Asia Minor. Consequently the type which Strzygowski classifies as specifically Armenian appears at a later date in Armenia than elsewhere.[1] Nevertheless there are certain factors to be taken into consideration on the other side. It is quite evident that the Armenian architects showed a marked predilection for domed churches, and the vaulted basilica without a dome was an alien form which disappeared as soon as Greek and Syrian influences waned. The domed square was in use

[1] cf. Sirarpie Der Nersessian, *Armenia and the Byzantine Empire*, 1945, p. 58.

before the seventh century, and the variety and complexity of the extant monuments show that they are not initial attempts but the result of experiments over a long period of time. Of particular importance in this connexion are the church at Awan, built by the Catholicos John of Bagaran (590–611), and the church of Phghni founded by Manuel Amatuni in the first half of the sixth century. Finally there is the literary evidence which indicates that the word 'dome' is of frequent occurrence in the Armenian writings e.g. the LXX translation of Haggai 1.4 used the words οἴκοις κοιλοστάθμοις, with coffered ceilings; in the Armenian text this becomes 'domed houses'.[1] However, Strzygowski's theory remains at best an unsupported hypothesis and while it must be admitted that Armenian architecture was never a mere provincial expression of Byzantine art but revealed a vigorous originality, the dearth of evidence, coupled with the fact that the squinch rather than the pendentive would have evolved from wooden corbelling, make it necessary to look elsewhere for tangible information which may help to solve the problem.

The third theory to be considered is that of Choisy, who argued that the pendentive was a creation of builders in Anatolia,[2] arising out of the practice of constructing vaults from thin bricks laid on edge. The first course was tilted inwards in order to embed it more firmly into the wall, the second course rested upon the first and was also tilted and so the process was continued until the barrel vault was complete. The next development was the cross vault over a square, and this could be raised in height until it became a domical vault with continuous pendentives. Influenced by Mesopotamia and Iran the Anatolians adopted this method and discovered the pendentive. This hypothesis is all the more ingenious because once again there is no direct evidence to support it, and it is rather a reconstruction of how the pendentive may have evolved than a certain statement of where in fact it did originate.

It is time to leave these speculations since there is one

[1] Der Nersessian, *op. cit.*, p. 59.   [2] *L'art de bâtir chez les Byzantins*, 1883.

country in which there are early and numerous examples of
the pendentive, a fact which at least strongly suggests, even
though it may not actually prove, that this was the place
where it was first devised, and that is Syria. Thus at Kusr-en-
Nueijis there are spherical pendentives in the Palace of the
Princes, dating from the latter part of the second century;
there are others in the baths at Gerasa which are not later
than the first half of the third century; yet another specimen
is to be found in a pagan tomb at Samaria which is of the end
of the second century or the beginning of the third, and in
the third century Baths of Brad in North Syria there are also
continuous pendentives.[1] When it is recalled that the earliest
known use of them outside Syria is at the end of the fourth
century in the mausoleum of St Menas at Maryūt, and that it
is not found in the mountains of Asia Minor before the tenth
century, there is every reason to agree with Creswell's
conclusion that Syria was the place of its origin since 'a
series of examples, perfect in theoretical conception and
practical execution, beginning in the second century A.D. is
to be found there'.[2] The most likely process of development
therefore, as far as it can be reconstructed, is that the dome
on squinches developed in Sassanian Persia and Altai-Iran,
passed eventually into Syria where native architects con-
trived the spherical pendentive, possibly aided in their
solution by experiments carried out in Armenia.

The dome over a square became the characteristic and
essential feature of Byzantine church building, being used
with various elaborations. In its simplest form it appeared
either as the domed square which became the quatrefoil of
Armenia, or as the domed hall church in which the piers
supporting the dome were applied directly to the exterior
walls, the aisles being suppressed and surviving only as
recesses without any independent function.

The domed basilica, a type almost exclusively confined to
Asia and the Balkans, is a combination, as its name indicates,
of the domical superstructure with the basilical ground plan;
it is therefore probably another example of the attempted

[1] Creswell, *op. cit.*, I, pp. 313ff.   [2] *op. cit.*, p. 323.

fusion between the centralized martyrium and the rectangular church. It is likely that this type originated in Anatolia—at all events the earliest examples are to be found in that area. At Khodja Kalessi, on the slopes of the Colycadnus valley in Cilicia, there is a domed basilica of the first half of the fifth century; it has a nave terminating in an enclosed apse and two aisles with galleries (*Fig 23*). At

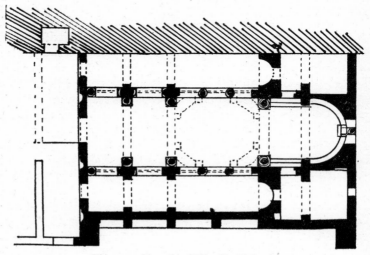

Fig. 23. Church of Khodja Kalessi.

Meriamlik, three miles north of Seleucia, there is another fifth-century church, possibly erected by the Emperor Zeno in 470, which consists of two bays flanked by galleried aisles; the eastern bay was covered with a dome and a polygonal apse was placed at the eastern extremity. Of the same period is the so-called double church at Ephesus and probably also the church of St Sophia at Salonika, the masonry of which appears to be of the fifth century.[1] This last building has been reproduced, with some modifications, at Ḳaṣr Ibn Wardân in north-east Syria where the church, a combination of the dome with the three-aisled basilica, is evidently the product of strong Byzantine influence. The

[1] J. A. Hamilton, *op. cit.*, p. 39.

central square over which the dome was to be placed was
lengthened towards the east and west by walls carrying
tunnel vaults. The spaces above the springing of these vaults
were filled in to form a solid rectangle which was flat on top;
from this, on the exterior, rose an octagon which carried the
circular dome on pendentives. At the east end there is an
inscribed apse, flanked by chambers communicating directly
with the side aisles; these open into the central space by
three arcades carried on two columns, and return across the

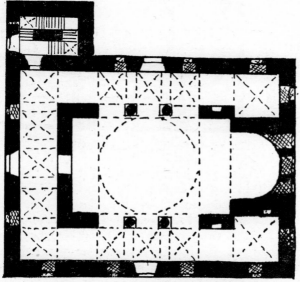

Fig. 24. Church of Ḳaṣr Ibn Wardân.

west end to form an interior narthex. A staircase built at the
north-west corner of the church leads up to the gallery above
the side aisles and narthex. The side chambers, aisles, narthex
and gallery all have domed cross vaults of brick set between
wide transverse arches (*Fig. 24*). The church of St Irene at
Constantinople, as it now stands, is a cross-domed basilica,
i.e. it is basilical on the ground but cruciform at gallery
level where the north and south arches are prolonged as
barrel vaults over the aisles to the outside walls; originally,

as erected under Justinian, it was probably a domed basilica, complete with narthex and preceded by an atrium.

The supreme example of the domed basilica is the great church of St Sophia at Constantinople (*Fig. 25*). This was

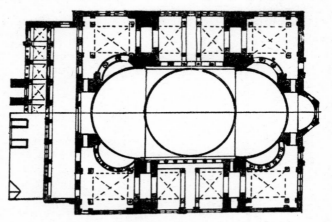

Fig. 25. St Sophia, Constantinople.

built upon a site previously occupied by a Theodosian basilica built in 415 to replace the church of Constantius which had been destroyed by fire eleven years earlier after standing for only forty years.[1] The new church was dedicated on the twenty-sixth of December, 537, in the eleventh year of Justinian. Twenty-one years later an earthquake damaged the main dome which, in the course of the repair work, was raised twenty feet, the church being reopened after an interval of five years on Christmas Eve, 563.[2] Three contemporary authors have left descriptions of it as it appeared after its restoration, Paulus Silentarius, who was one of the court officials, Agathias, a native of Asia Minor, and Evagrius who was born at Epiphania on the Orontes.[3] From these accounts it is possible to form a vivid

[1] Sven Larsen, 'A Forerunner of Hagia Sophia', *A.J.A.*, XLI, 1937, pp. 1–5.
[2] cf. Theophanes, *Chronographia*.
[3] W. R. Lethaby and Harold Swainson, *The Church of Sancta Sophia Constantinople. A Study of Byzantine Building*, 1894.

VII. S. Sophia

VIII. S. Sophia, looking towards apse

picture of this masterpiece, which, although still standing, was converted into a Turkish mosque, losing much of its splendour in the process, and in 1935 was transformed into a Byzantine museum of art. The great dome, 'the deep bosomed swelling roof' in the words of Paulus, which resembles 'the encircling heavens' (ll. 530–1) is 107 feet in diameter. It shares the four massive piers on which it rests with two semi-domes, one to the east and the other to the west, which serve as buttresses, themselves supported at one end by two niches and the apse, and at the other by a corresponding pair of niches and a double narthex. To north and south the dome is buttressed by solid arches, pierced with windows, the space between the arches being filled in with pendentives, 'for where, as needs must be, the arches bend away from one another, and would have shown empty air, a curved wall, like a triangle, grows over touching the rim of the arches on either side. And the four triangles, creeping over, spread out, until they become united above the crown of each arch. The middle portion of the arches, as much as forms the curved rim, the builders' skill has formed with thin bricks, and have thus made fast the topmost curves of the house of stone' (ll. 469–76). The nave is flanked by lofty columns of Thessalonian marble, four in the lower and six in the upper storey, the *gynaeceum* or women's gallery, separating it from the aisles, the whole building being enclosed by a rectangle broken by the apse at the east end. 'Looking towards the sunset one might see the same as towards the dawn, though a portion differs. For there in the centre it is not drawn round in a circle, as on the eastern boundary, where sit the learned priests on seats of resplendent silver, but at the west end is a vast entrance; not only one door but three. And outside the doors there stretches a long porch, receiving under its wide portals those that enter in, as long as the wondrous shrine of the church is broad. This place is called by the Greeks narthex. Here through the night, a melodious sound, constantly rising, soothes the ears of Christ the Benefactor, where the sacred psalms of God-fearing David are sung by priests in alternate verses [i.e.

[71]

antiphonally] . . . into this porch open seven wide holy gates calling the people within in hosts' (ll. 417–440). In front of this exo-narthex there is an atrium surrounded by cloisters with a bubbling fountain in the centre.

The architects of St Sophia were Anthemius of Tralles and Isidore of Miletus, but their Asiatic origin does not necessarily involve an oriental outlook, since Miletus was a Hellenistic coast town and Tralles, a little way up the Maeander valley, was subject to the same influences. Strzygowski however argues for a preponderance of Eastern conceptions, regarding the church as a development of the Armenian quatrefoil with ambulatory, in which the dome rests on the wedge-like projections of the walls between each pair of niches. The dome of St Sophia is, according to him, typically Armenian being abutted by two semidomes, (i.e. niche buttresses), the only essentially Greek feature being the gallery. Diehl on the other hand considers that the semi-domes were achieved by bisecting the domed centralized plan, pushing the half domes outwards and inserting another dome. Others see in it the elaboration of the niches used in round buildings, of the type already considered in connexion with St Vitale. The second and third of these theories need not detain us long: Diehl's solution is ingenious but unconvincing; architecture in this period reveals a steady development, which is achieved not by a scissors and paste method but by the bringing together of different forms, the creative task consisting in fusing them into a harmonious whole; the keynote is combination, not the cutting up of different elements in order to reassemble them in a new pattern. The derivation from semi-circular niches and recesses through St Vitale and SS Sergius and Bacchus is equally doubtful; it has already been emphasized that the niches in these two buildings are primarily decorative and not functional, but in St Sophia the semi-domes and the secondary semi-domes which surmount the niches are used as buttresses, suggesting that Strzygowski's theory is indeed the correct one. It must however be recognized that St Sophia is not merely the transportation to Constantinople of the old Armenian unity of the apse buttressed dome, exactly as it was known in the country of its origin. One has only to compare the churches at Mastara and Awan with St Sophia to realise that the last is no slavish imitation of Armenian prototypes, however dependent it may be on them for its constituent elements.

It is immediately obvious that the express aim of Anthemius and Isidore was to adapt the dome to the fundamental scheme of the basilica; the existence of the great atrium in front of the church is ample evidence for this. It will be recalled that in the centralized martyria the vertical axis predominates, while in the basilica it is the horizontal that is emphasized. In St Sophia the merging of the semi-domes with the central dome by the spherical surfaces of the pendentives to produce the effect of a long elliptical dome, and the omission of any drum—thus depressing the roof and preventing it soaring to too great a height—provided loftiness and space. At the same time it preserved the horizontal perspective which accorded so well with the liturgical action of which the building was intended to be the setting. But this combination, this fusion, was carried out in Byzantium, not in Armenia, and it seems only reasonable therefore to accept the simplest solution by saying with Millet that St Sophia is a synthesis of all previous types amongst which the Armenian quatrefoil may be legitimately included— a synthesis achieved by architects of genius whose inspiration, free from any plagiarism, created a building as bold and noble in its conception as in its construction.[1] No attempt, however, was made by later architects to imitate this magnificent plan, and the type which eventually became universal in the East was not the domed basilica but the cruciform church of which there were two principal forms: the free-standing cross and the inscribed cross.

The free-standing cross, in which the thrust of the central dome is taken by the walls inscribing the cross, had the shape either of the *crux immissa* or Latin Cross, or of the *crux commissa* which resembles the letter T. Just as the round

[1] W. R. Zaloziecky, *Die Sophienkirche in Konstantinopel und ihre Stellung in der Geschichte des Abedandlandischen Architektur,* 1936.

[73]

and octagonal buildings were originally commemorative so also was the cruciform, and it appears to have been an imitation of subterranean tombs. The belief in the resurrection of the flesh so influenced the early Christians that they did all in their power to safeguard their mortal remains

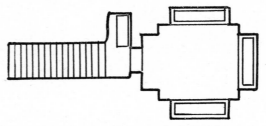

Fig. 26. Cruciform tomb, Sokhani.

in anticipation of the Last Day. Those in the East who could afford it had their tombs hewed out of the rock, confident that these at least would prove indestructible, and they sought further protection by invoking fierce curses upon any

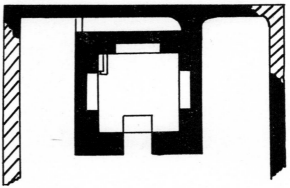

Fig. 27. Mausoleum, Philippeville.

who might seek to disturb their rest.[1] These grottos were usually square, the entrance door being in one side, and in the three others recesses or *arcosolia* to receive the sarcophagi; this produced a cruciform plan (*Fig. 26*) which may be seen

[1] A. Parrot, *Malédictions et violations des tombes*, 1939, p. 178.

IX. Rotunda of S. George, Salonika

X. Interior of church at Mshabbak, looking towards apse

time and again in the catacombs of Alexandria, Palmyra and
Sidon.[1] This plan was later transferred to the open air and
was reproduced, for example, in the great pagan mausoleum
at Seidnaya near Damascus[2] or that at Philippeville in North
Africa (*Fig. 27*). Christians accustomed to look upon the
cross as the sign of salvation would easily recognize it in this

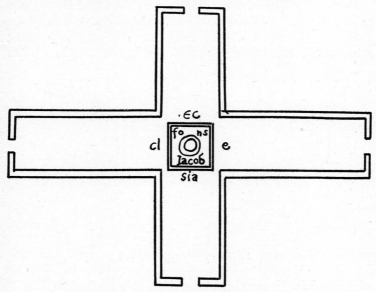

Fig. 28. The well of Jacob, Shechem.

plan and, emphasizing its outlines, they adopted it for
religious buildings and in particular for martyria. Thus it
appeared in the martyrium of St Babylas, erected on the
outskirts of Antioch by Meletius in 381.[3] This consists of
a central square, covered with a wooden pyramidal roof,
from the sides of which radiate the arms of a cross. A similar
building was that erected to enshrine the well of Jacob at
Shechem, known from a drawing made by Arculfus in the
seventh century (*Fig. 28*). To the north, in Asia Minor, there

[1] J. Strzygowski, *Kleinasien*, 1903, p. 135.
[2] Lassus, *op. cit,,* p. 119.   [3] *Antioch-on-the-Orontes, op. cit.*, pp. 5ff.

is a profusion of T-shaped cruciform buildings upon almost every hill top of the Kara Dagh; this multiplicity of small shrines was probably due to the influence of polytheism, the Christian saints replacing the pagan gods, and the summits of the mountains, always an object of awe in the East, being reconsecrated by martyria.

In the West the free-standing cross only appeared where oriental influences were predominant, as at Ravenna where the mausoleum of Galla Placidia (*c.* 450) had four vaulted arms connected at the centre by a dome (*Fig. 29*); this

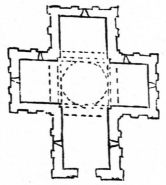

Fig. 29. Galla Placidia, Ravenna.

edifice originally stood in the vicinity of a large church, also cruciform, which was dedicated to the Holy Cross, a further example of the way in which memorial buildings influenced the congregational church. Its congregational use in the East was not widespread, and there were few if any imitations of Justinian's church of the Holy Apostles with which he replaced the Constantinian octagon erected by the emperor as a mausoleum for himself and his family; the sixth-century church seems to have had five domes, one in the centre and the others distributed along the arms of the cross,[1] of which the western one was probably lengthened by an additional

[1] The church erected by St Ambrose at Milan in 383 (originally dedicated to the Apostles and later to St Nazarius) seems also to have been a free-standing cross.

[76]

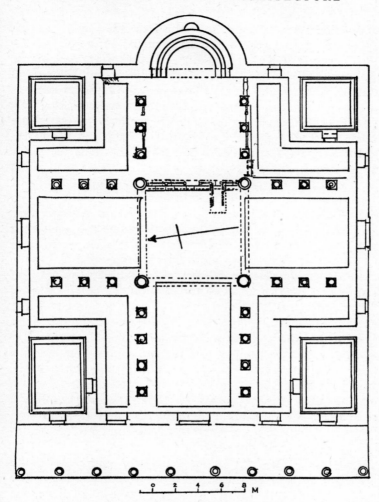

Fig. 30. Prophets, Apostles and Martyrs, Gerasa.

bay, as in the church of the Prophets, Apostles and Martyrs at Gerasa (*Fig. 30*).[1]

[1] J. W. Crowfoot, *Churches at Jerash, British School of Archaeology in Jerusalem, Supplementary Papers*, 3, 1931, p. 31.

There are two other churches which must be mentioned in connexion with this survey of the free standing cross, viz. that of St Simeon the Stylite constructed at the end of the fifth century at Kal'at Sim'ân, and that of St Simeon the Younger at Jebel Sim'ân between Antioch and Seleucia at the end of the sixth century. These are two further examples of the architect's endeavour to combine martyria and basilicas, and indeed the architect of the first of them attempted to fuse three different types: the octagon, the cross and the three-aisled basilica. The column upon which the saint passed his days stood in the centre of an octagonal open court which itself was the centre of a free-standing cross composed of four three-aisled basilicas, the eastern one having three projecting apses.[1] The column of St Simeon the Younger was similarly placed in the centre of an octagon from which radiated the four arms of a cross, but the north, south and west arms were corridors, although the last, which led to the main door, contained porticos and so assumed the basilical form. The eastern part of the monument consisted of a basilica flanked by two others, the whole complex being enclosed in a rectangle.[2] From this brief description it will be evident that the architects, in effect, gave up the attempt to achieve an organic unity out of the two elements with which they were presented, viz. the martyrium and the basilica, and, instead of combining them, contented themselves with placing them in juxtaposition. This elementary solution recalls the Constantinian monuments at Jerusalem and Bethlehem, where the memorial and congregational buildings were not fused but remained side by side.

The second main type of cruciform church was the inscribed cross or cross-in-square,[3] so-called because, as the thrust of the dome is distributed over the whole edifice, the walls of the cross are no longer needed and are replaced by

[1] M. Ecochard, 'Le Sanctuaire de Qal'at Sem'ân'. *Bulletin d'Etudes orientales*, VI, 1936; D. Krencker, *Die Wallfahrtkirchen des Simeon Stylites in Kal'at Sim'an. Ergebnisse von Untersuchungen im Frühjahr 1938, Forschritte und Forschungen*, 1939.

[2] G. de Jerphanion, 'Sur l'église de Saint-Symeon Stylite au Djebel Sem'ân', *Orientalia Christiana Periodica*, IX, 1943.

[3] Sometimes referred to as the *crux quadrata* or Greek cross.

transverse arches on piers or columns. The angles between the arms of the cross are filled up so that a square plan is obtained at ground level, but the roof of the angle spaces being lower than the rest the cruciform plan is evident above. The dome may rest either on two piers and on the antennae of the apse, or on four central piers—with or without an additional bay between the eastern arm—or have a lower one of its own.[1] The origin of this plan has been hotly debated, and it has been suggested that the cross-in-square developed from the domed basilica with pendentives. As the arches north and south of the central dome proved inadequate to counteract its thrust, they were prolonged as barrel vaults to the outside walls, thus forming the cross-domed basilica. The galleries were then suppressed, with the consequent lowering of the aisles, and the nave was shortened to produce the obscured cross. At best this remains an unsupported theory, since the dating of the domed basilica is uncertain and no transitional forms, apart from the cross-domed basilica, are extant. There are however numerous buildings, although most of them are not of an early date, which suggest that the cross-in-square evolved naturally from the free-standing cross; these are cruciform churches with the four angles filled in, but the angle-spaces have no constructional purpose in that they do not take any of the thrust of the central dome, e.g. the church dedicated to the Prophets, Apostles and Martyrs at Gerasa; it was built in 464 and has the form of a Latin cross with the angle-spaces filled in with chambers (*Fig. 30*).[2] It is obvious how simple it would be to transform these into buttresses for the vaults of the arms of the cross, which is the function they fulfil in the compact unity of the cross-in-square. With this solution Strzygowski is not satisfied, and finds the home of this type in Armenia, where he declares it has originated directly from the niche-buttressed square with interior supports through the dropping of the niche buttresses and a slight increase of nave length. It must be granted that the cross-in-square is

[1] *vide* Hamilton, *op. cit.*, pp. 21–23.
[2] J. W. Crowfoot, *Early Churches in Palestine*, 1941, pp. 85–8.

the typical form of Armenian architecture, but that is by no means certain evidence that Armenia was its place of origin. More recent research has thrown new light on this question and it is now evident that the cross-in-square is closely connected with certain types of temple which are to be found in the region to the south east of the Mediterranean and also with the οἶκοι τετραστύλοι of Hellenistic architecture.[1] The most celebrated of these prototypes is the Tychaion of Mismiyeh which combines a tripartite sanctuary with the plan of the inscribed cross.[2] The Church was no doubt induced to adopt this form by its similarity to those tombs in which a cross was inscribed in a square by means of solid angles.

The influence of these funerary monuments and above all of the developing cult of the saints was thus responsible for the production of almost every type of centralized building and then eventually for the ousting of the basilica from its place of pre-eminence in the East. While in the West the basilica, with its confessio, continued in use for many centuries, it was the cross-in-square which finally became the consecrated church form of Eastern Orthodoxy, and was preserved by it through the centuries of the Byzantine era until at the Renaissance it too crossed the Mediterranean to Italy and beyond.

[1] J. Lassus, 'Deux églises cruciformes du Hauran', *Bulletin d'Etudes Orientales*, I, 1932.

[2] A.-S. Keck, 'The Tychaion of Phaena-Mismiyeh', *A.J.A.*, XLV, 1941, pp. 98ff.

IV

THE ORIENTATION
AND FURNITURE OF
THE CHURCH

THE ORIENTATION of the different types of church was from the middle of the fourth century practically uniform, with the apse at the east end. The earliest buildings which have been preserved, however, those of the Constantinian period, have their sanctuary at the west end and it has therefore been assumed that this was the primitive custom and that it prevailed until a few years after the death of the first Christian emperor. Against this theory certain legitimate objections may be brought. In the first place, the fact that the earliest known churches have western apses is no certain evidence for those which existed before them. Indeed, such literary references as there are suggest the contrary. Tertullian records the pagan accusation that Christians were sun-worshippers, commenting that 'the idea has no doubt originated from our being known to turn to the East in prayer.'[1] Clement of Alexandria in like manner affirms: 'in correspondence with the manner of the sun's rising, prayers are made looking towards the sunrise in the east. Whence also the most ancient temples looked towards the west, that people might be taught to turn to the east when facing the images'.[2] In the second place those churches which have a western sanctuary were all built either directly or indirectly under the influence of the Emperor Constantine: St Peter's, St Paul's, St Lorenzo, the Anastasis and the basilicas at Tyre and Antioch. It is

[1] *Apol.*, xvi. [2] *Strom.*, VII. 7.

[81]

reasonable to suppose therefore that their direction was due to some whim of the emperor himself. It is to be noted that for eight years after the battle of the Milvian Bridge the imperial mints continued to issue coins in honour of the Unconquered Sun, one of them not ceasing the issue until 323; further the emperor's legislation on Sunday observance in 321 refers to Sunday as 'the day celebrated by the veneration of the Sun'. Thus for many years after he had become the official patron of Christianity, Constantine preserved traces of his earlier sun worship, and this would account for his predilection for churches with apses at the west end. The orientation to which the *Apostolic Constitutions* bear witness in the middle of the fourth century[1] would then not be an innovation but a reversion to the earlier practice. Some support for this contention is provided by the house church at Dura-Europos; the room used for liturgical gatherings has a raised platform at the east end, on which the altar was no doubt placed. Whereas the small community made use of the house as it stood, and its orientation is therefore a matter of chance, it would nevertheless have been possible for them to have constructed the bema at the west end of the room, but this has been deliberately avoided. Hence the sole surviving example of a pre-Constantinian church had its sanctuary at the east end. There is no need to account for this orientation by asserting with Strzygowski the influence of Armenia and its Mazdean sun temples.[2] Clement of Alexandria provides sufficient ground for its adoption when he says: 'the east is an image of the day of birth, and from that point the light which has shone forth at first from the darkness increases, there has also dawned on those involved in darkness a day of the knowledge of truth'.[3] In close harmony with this is the reference to Christ as the 'Dayspring from on high' and the

[1] II. 57

[2] J. Strzygowski, *L'ancien art chrétien de Syrie*. At the same time it is probable that the custom was oriental in origin, the Eastern Church keeping more rigidly to the rule than the West where many early churches in Rome conform to no rule whatsoever, e.g. St Maria Maggiore which is north-west, St Sabina north-east, and St Agnese south-east.

[3] *loc. cit.*

'Light of the World' to which Chrysostom calls the attention of his hearers.[1] Other reasons for or, more correctly, deductions from the practice are that in praying to the east the soul is hoping for restoration to its ancient home in Paradise through Christ the Second Adam,[2] and that Christians are looking for their Lord's return, since the coming of the Son of Man will be like the 'lightning that cometh out of the east and shineth even unto the west.'[3]

It was however very rarely that the longitudinal axis of the church lay directly east and west; in many Syrian churches the variation is as much as twelve degrees to the south side of a line drawn at right angles to the true north. It has been suggested that the change was due to the attempt to conform to the position occupied by the rising sun on the day of the patronal festival, but where it has been possible to test this hypothesis, as for the basilica of St Salsa at Tipasa, there has been found no concordance between the orientation of the building and the rising of the sun.[4] In all probability the variations signified nothing and were due to the inaccuracy of the instruments employed, especially as two churches in Syria, both erected within seventeen years of each other, both by the same architect, both of approximately the same size and both finished in the month of August show a difference of five degrees in their orientation.[5]

Whatever the direction of the church, once the doors had been passed it was towards the altar that attention was focused. Its position was not immediately stereotyped, although frequently it was placed upon the chord of the apse. However, in most Grecian churches and in many African churches it is found in front of it, as in the three basilicas at Thelepte, while in Damous-el-Karita at Carthage it was almost in the centre of the church, being some twenty-five yards from the apse. In some Syrian churches the altar stood

[1] *Homil. in Zach.*, vi. 12.
[2] Basil, *De Sp. Sanct.*, 27.   [3] Hilar., *in Ps*. lxvii.
[4] S. Gsell, *Les Monuments antiques de l'Algérie*, II, 1901, p. 124, n. 2. cf. R. de Lasteyrie, 'La direction de l'axe de l'église est-elle symbolique?', *Bulletin Monumental*, 1906.
[5] H. C. Butler, *Early Churches in Syria*, 1929, p. 182.

at the back of the apse; at Zerzita, for example, it was placed
against the wall into which architraves from the two columns
of the ciborium were inserted; at Brad and in a chapel at
Kharâb Shems the altar was so situated that the so-called
basilical position of the celebrant would have been impossible.[1] All these differences in location indicate divergences
in liturgical practice which, during the early centuries, was
by no means uniform.

The use of altars by Christians in the second century was
denied by the pagans, who considered that this affirmation
substantiated their repeated accusations of atheism. Admittedly the primitive Christian altar had little in common
with the Jewish or pagan altars which were intended for
bloody sacrifices, but Ireneaus testifies quite definitely to
their existence and use,[2] and the absence of any primitive
examples is readily accounted for since they were ordinary
perishable wooden tables of no uniform size or shape.[3]
Wooden altars indeed continued to be used for many
centuries, and Optatus records how the Donatists seized and
broke up one belonging to the Catholics[4] while Augustine
recounts the unfortunate adventures of Bishop Maximianus
who was almost beaten to death with boards from a destroyed
altar.[5] Gradually however the Church came to discriminate
in favour of altars of stone; undoubtedly this was in the main
due to the use of altar tombs in the catacombs. In many of the
subterranean chambers there is one principal tomb cut out
of the tufa and surmounted by a vault; a marble flagstone, in
which several bronze rings were fastened, was placed in
grooves over the tomb and could be pulled forward to act
as an altar for the memorial Eucharist. This usage spread
with such rapidity that we find the Council of Epaon in

---

[1] cf. Basilica A at Philippi, where the basilical position is rendered impossible
by the presence of an opening, down into the chamber containing the relics,
exactly where the officiant would have stood; as it is, he would have had to
stand with his back to the congregation; Lemerle, *Philippes*, p. 371.

[2] *Adv. Haer.*, IV. 18,6; cf. Ignatius, *Ad Ephes.*, 5; *Ad Trall.*, 7; *Ad Philad.*, 4.

[3] In the later catacomb frescoes a three-legged table is popular.

[4] *De Schism. Donat.*, I. vi. 1. [5] *Ep.*, clxxv. 7.

Gaul (517) prohibiting wooden altars altogether (canon 26).

At first it was customary to copy the wooden prototypes, and the numerous examples which have been preserved from the fifth century faithfully reproduce the table form. The altar found by Galla Placidia in St Giovanni Evangelista at Ravenna was supported on five legs, while that in the great basilica at Nikopolis in Greece had nine legs, three at each end and three across the centre; another from southern France (St Quenin, now at Vaison) has four miniature Corinthian columns as legs and along the front edge is a central monogram flanked by doves and the vine; a third from Auriol, also in southern France, has only one support.[1] Evidence of the use of a single pedestal is also forthcoming from Syria where a semi-circular altar was sometimes employed;[2] undoubtedly this form derives from the sigma which from the third century A.D. was to be found in almost every triclinium throughout the empire. The development of the cult of relics, however, led to a modification and in the sixth century there was a change from an open to a solid altar, from a table to a boxlike structure.[3]

After the Peace of the Church basilicas in the West were built above the tombs of the Apostles and martyrs. In Rome this involved the destruction of whole galleries of the catacombs; in the provinces this connecting of the altar with the relics involved less excavation, and Etheria records how a church was built at the burial place of Job near Carneas 'in such a manner that the stone with the body should not be moved, but that it should be placed, where the body had been found, and that the body should lie under the altar'.[4] A vertical shaft connected the tomb with the holy table and access to it was obtained by means of an opening in the side of the altar facing the body of the church; this opening was closed by a grating of stone or metal which was called the

---

[1] Another example has been found at Sardis in Asia Minor.

[2] J. Sauvaget, *Inventaire des monuments de Damas*, 1932, pp. 52, 78.

[3] *vide* J. Barnea, Τό παλαιοχριστιανικόν Θυσιαστήριον, Θεολογική Βιβλιοθήκη, No. 5, Athens, 1940.

[4] *Pilgrimage*, trans. by M. I. M'Clure and C. O. Feltoe, 1921, p. 30.

fenestella confessionis. The term *confessio* itself was originally employed to designate the place where a martyr had witnessed to his faith by the shedding of his blood. Sometimes the body was buried on the very spot, at others it was transported to a nearby crypt; in either case the tomb was the confessio. Eventually the name was applied to any sacred tomb placed beneath an altar, to the shaft connecting them and even to the altar itself. The pierced slab of the *fenestella* had an opening, usually closed by a door of silver or gold, large enough to allow the passage of an arm and by this means small objects, such as handkerchiefs, were brought into contact with the tomb; it was these *brandea* and *palliola* which in the first five centuries were exported as relics. In those churches where the saint's tomb was too far below the surface to be readily accessible perforated plates, *cataractae*, were inserted across the shaft, objects being placed on them. So when Justinian was erecting his Church of the Apostles at Constantinople he asked for some portion of the bodies of Peter and Paul; upon the refusal of Pope Hormisdas, he sent a second request that his relics might be laid on the *cataractam secundam*, on the lower plate.

Constantine showed a preference for a different plan, viz. a building in which the tomb was approached by staircases; this appears in the confessio of St Lawrence, and in the original church of the Nativity at Bethlehem, where steps led down to the holy grotto. Similar to this, though with an interesting peculiarity, was the fourth-century church erected at Rome in honour of St Valentine. As the saint's body was so placed that a superimposed building was out of the question, contrary to the usual custom, it was removed and a narrow gallery, like those of the catacombs but lined with marble, was constructed beneath the tribune; here immediately below the altar the tomb of the martyr was placed; steps from the side aisles descending into the primitive crypt.

Where a martyrium was already in existence to mark the resting place of the saint, it was sometimes the practice to build an adjacent basilica for congregational purposes, the apse of which met that of the earlier shrine and was pierced with a window so that the worshippers could see the chapel through the perforated stone window plates (*transennae*). This was the plan adopted in the construction of St Sinforosa (fourth century), which is a modest form of the arrangement, described by Paulinus, of St Felix at Nola which had three arches pierced through the apse so that there might be a free prospect across the covered court which separated the two basilicas. This triple arch was copied by other architects and is to be found, for example, in the fourth-century basilica Severiana at Naples.[1] From a passage in the *Liber Pontificalis*, in the acts of Paschal I, it seems that the tribune of St Maria Maggiore was also anciently constructed with open arches; these, however, communicated not with an oratory but with an ambulatory which was apparently used as a matroneum, i.e. a place reserved for women.[2]

There were of course many churches dedicated in honour of saints whose bodies rested elsewhere. Accordingly the practice arose of enclosing in the altar some small relics, such as brandea, i.e. strips of linen which had touched the tomb of a martyr,[3] in which case not only was a box form essential, but it was customary to inscribe on the altar an inventory of what it contained. An interesting example of this is the altar in the basilica at Henchir-el-Begueur, in the region of Tebessa. In the centre of its upper surface is a cylindrical cavity surrounded by a groove in which a square covering was inserted; the relics which this originally contained were those of St Montanus who died at Carthage in the year 259; on the front of the altar there is a monogrammatic cross with the A and ω and a panel with the inscription—

MEMORIA
SACTIMO
NTANI

---

[1] *vide* Lowrie, *op. cit.*, Fig. 40, p. 127.

[2] Women were separated from men in the congregation, either sitting on one side of the nave or in the gynaeceum or gallery which extended above the side aisles and narthex.

[3] cf. Gregory, *Ep.*, I. 4,30.

A second panel, now defaced, probably mentioned other relics. The form of the cross and of the letters and the abbreviation s$\overline{\text{A}}$cti indicate the sixth century.[1] It was this cult of relics which eventually led to there being more than one altar in a church, additional altars coming into use about the beginning of the fifth century, at first in side chapels and later in the church itself.

In the East the confessio scarcely appears, and the cult of the saints, as already mentioned, developed independently of the Eucharist in the martyria, which were separate buildings of the centralized type. In North Syria when the sacred relics were brought within the precincts of the basilica, a practice which was initiated during the second decade of the fifth century, it was customary to place them in one of the side chambers, flanking the apse, usually, though not invariably, on the south side. Access to this chapel was obtained by means of an arch, from the keystone of which hung an oil lamp above a transverse beam resting on the pilasters; from this curtains were suspended. In the chapel against the east wall and sometimes beneath a baldachin was the reliquary containing the mortal remains of the saint. Other furniture in the chamber included cupboards, which contained either other relics or those things necessary for the cult, stone benches and holy water stoups. The reliquaries themselves, of which a number have been discovered,[2] took the form of a miniature stone sarcophagus with a gable lid. Through this covering a hole was pierced by means of which oil could be introduced, and a corresponding outlet provided with a metal tap was made in the base in order that the liquid might be drawn off. This was the holy oil, the oil of the martyrs, to which the fathers make frequent reference;[3] it was preserved by the pilgrims in little flasks or *ampullae*. This use of reliquaries was by no means confined to Syria, other examples having been discovered in Palestine and also in Asia Minor. But the Western practice of bringing the cult

[1] *vide Bulletin de la Société des antiquaires de France*, 1880, p. 270.
[2] J. Lassus, *Inventaire archéologique de la région au Nord-Est de Harma*, 1935, 2 vols.
[3] e.g. Paulinus, *Carm.*, xviii. 38; xxi. 590; Theodoret, *H.E.*, xxi; *vide* Lassus, *Sanctuaires*, pp. 163ff.

of the saints and the celebration of the Eucharist into a close unity was destined to prevail over the Eastern separatist tendency. Already at Gerasa in the sixth-century church of St George the reliquary was placed either immediately behind or beneath the altar,[1] and this was a long step towards the Council of Nicaea in 787 which ordered the placing of relics beneath all altars.

Although the altar was the focal point of the liturgy no costly material was usually employed in its construction; partly perhaps through reverence for its traditional form and partly through the use of altar cloths. Constantine however presented St Peter's with a silver altar 'inlaid with gold, decorated with green and white jewels and jacinths on all sides, the number of the jewels being four hundred, the weight 350 lb.';[2] while Justinian gave a golden altar studded with precious stones to Sancta Sophia. But since altars generally continued to be of humble material and since they retained the same limited dimensions, it became necessary, in the larger basilicas, if the altar were to remain the architectural centre of the building, to supply it with some costly and elaborate setting. Accordingly in the fourth century an ancient pagan custom was adopted, viz. the placing of a baldachin or ciborium over the altar. This was carried on four pillars; in the East it took the form of a cupola and hence its name κιβώριον, a cup; in the West it was more usual to have a conical or pyramidal roof. The ciborium was surmounted either by architraves on which the canopy directly rested, or by arches the angles of which were filled in to provide a horizontal basis for the covering. The first ciborium of which there is mention is that given by Constantine to the Lateran basilica. It was probably carried on four marble columns and weighed 2,025 lb. Facing the nave was a seated figure of Christ, 5 feet in height and weighing 120 lb., flanked by two Apostles each 5 feet tall and 90 lb. in weight; along the sides were disposed the remaining Apostles and at the rear facing the apse was another seated Christ with two angels, weighing 105 lb. each and holding rods, one to His

[1] *Gerasa*, p. 183.   [2] *Liber Pontificalis, Vita Sylv.*

right and one to His left. The canopy itself was of the purest gold. This ciborium was carried off by the Visigoths at the beginning of the fifth century, but Sixtus III (432–40) persuaded the Emperor Valentinian to erect a new one of which all that is known is that it was of silver and of approximately the same weight. Other ciboria are depicted in the mosaics of St George, Salonika: they are carried on spiral shafts with Byzantine capitals. According to Agnellus the Basilica Ursiana at Ravenna had a silver ciborium erected by its bishop Victor (539–46) to replace a wooden one; this was preserved until the sixteenth century, being destroyed in 1512. Finally mention should be made of the ciborium in St Sophia which lasted until the thirteenth century. The magnificent canopy, vividly described by Paulus Silentarius, was raised on four silver columns which supported four arches; above these rose an octagonal cone on the apex of which was a bowl, its edges curving back like leaves, containing a globe surmounted by a cross. Round the base of the cone were moulded acanthus leaves wreathed round eight hemispheres each containing five silver lamps.

None of these early ciboria are extant, the earliest dating from the ninth century, but those that do survive adhere sufficiently to the ancient type to give some indication of the splendour with which the altar was frequently surrounded.

The dignity of the altar was further enhanced by a row of five or six great columns adorning the presbyterium, which they were not originally intended to delimit, and are therefore not to be confused with the *cancellus*. It was from this ornamental feature that the *iconostasis* developed[1] and

[1] Lassus (*Sanctuaires*, p. 179) suggests that the beams placed across the arches opening into the chapels of the martyrs in many Syrian churches may have been decorated with images of the saints and that it was from this that the iconostasis developed; he admits that this is so far an unsupported hypothesis. According to A. Grabar (*Martyrium, Recherches sur le culte des reliques et l'art chrétien antique*, 1946, II, cap. viii) the predominating influence was the cult of relics; icons themselves being a development of the designs on the ampullae which contained *eulogiae*; the holy image eventually replacing the relic itself in the favour of the populace. cf. also I. B. Konstantynowicz, *Ikonstasis, Studien und Forschungen*, I, Lwow, 1939; L. Bréhier, 'Anciennes clôtures de choeur antérieures aux iconostases dans les monastères de l'Athos', *Studi Bizantini et Neoellenici*, VI, 2, 1940, pp. 93–105.

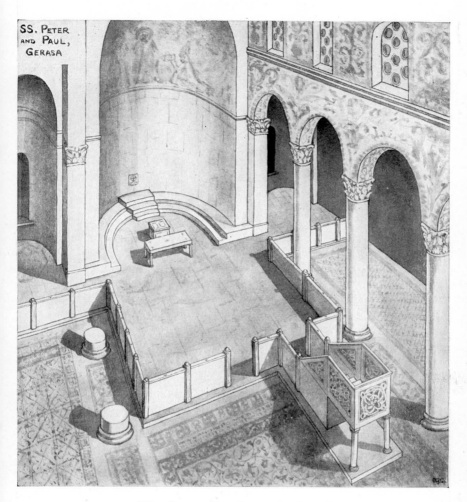

XI.   Restoration of an early chancel

XII.   Ivory throne of Maximian, Ravenna

although the term is formed of two Greek words, εἰκών and στάσις, and although it only applies at the present day to churches of the Eastern Orthodox communion, it was to be found in the West at an early period. In the catacomb of St Gennaro at Naples there is a primitive iconostasis cut out of the tufa, dating probably from the early fourth century; in the basilica of Reparatus at Orléansville, 475, there are traces of another, while the Constantinian basilica of St Peter was also embellished in like manner with six white marble columns which the emperor had brought from Greece. It is however of the iconostasis of St Sophia that the fullest description has been preserved; this consisted of six pairs of silver-plated columns connected by screens of the same precious metal; it separated the bema from the *solea* or choir, communication between the two being by means of two silver doors.[1] This partition certainly marked the limits of the sanctuary, and as such may be compared to an elaborate cancellus.

Cancelli, made of wood, marble or metal, were used by the pagans in pre-Christian times; they were balustrades which both marked out the confines of an area and prevented ready access to it. They were used to define and protect orators' platforms and the seats of the magistrates. On the Triumphal Arch of Constantine the emperor is depicted behind cancelli which stretched in front of the rostra in the forum. In the Christian basilica these open-work balustrades enclosed that part of the church reserved for the clergy and also fenced off a portion for the Virgins.[2] They were employed in the catacombs, too, to protect the relics of the martyrs from the avidity of the faithful, and so in Praetextatus there is a niche enclosed by a transenna of open work marble.[3] It was this open work that was the common method of decorating cancelli in the fourth century, the stone being pierced to display a geometrical design. But in

[1] Paulus Silentarius, ll. 673–719.

[2] Ambrose, *De lapsu virginis consecratae*, vi.

[3] The terms *transenna* and *cancellus* were often used interchangeably, but there is a difference, viz. the former was a grill closing a bay, niche or window while the latter was a proper free-standing balustrade.

the next hundred years it became the fashion to have solid cancelli ornamented with designs in relief of which the typical form, appearing repeatedly, consisted of six hearts arranged like the spokes of a wheel and surrounded by a circle of ribbon with two loose ends each terminating in another heart, the whole surmounted by a cross. In many Palestinian basilicas the chancel extended some distance into the body of the church, occupying as much as a third or even a quarter of the nave. It was to these rails, in the early centuries, that the faithful brought their offerings at the Eucharist. But in the second half of the sixth century, probably under Justin II (565–78), changes in the liturgy led to a transformation in the chancel; this was the introduction of the rite of the prothesis and the two entrances. In place of the long deep chancel a broad tripartite plan was adopted, the central portion containing the altar, that to the north being the chapel of the prothesis where the preparation took place, and the third section being the diaconicon. Both these flanking chambers were frequently provided with apses but these had no liturgical purpose. The church at 'Ain Hanniya, to the south-west of Jerusalem, reveals this process of transformation, for the mosaics in the aisles originally extended as far as the side chambers, while the chancel projected into the nave; but when the tripartite pattern was accepted it became necessary to raise the floors of the two bays to bring them up to the level of the central portion, an alteration which took place to the detriment of the mosaic scheme.[1] In Syria a considerable number of stone cancelli has been preserved, an especially fine example being the parapet in the fourth-century basilica at Zebed. Five carved stone panels were held in place by rectangular posts; the panels had raised frames and the sunken portions were ornamented with various designs in low relief.[2] On the frames were inscriptions, running across the tops and down the sides; according to one of them 'Rabula made the throne', i.e. the bishop's seat. Few traces of these seats have been found

[1] J. W. Crowfoot, *Early Churches in Palestine*, 1941, p. 52.
[2] H. C. Butler, *Architecture and other Arts*, 1904, pp. 302–3.

in Syria but this inscription indicates that they were in use and in Eusebius there is the expresssion, βῆμα καί θρόνος ὕψηλος, to designate the episcopal chair of Paul of Samosata.[1]

In the West the term cathedra was employed, another Greek word which referred originally to any kind of chair, being applied to the θρόνος with a straight high back, to the δίφρος, a kind of stool, and to the κλισμός with a concave back. They were made of marble or wood, the senatorial cathedrae being veneered with ivory; cushions and draperies added to the comfort and it was in wide use in the early days of the Empire. At a later period it was adopted almost exclusively by the rhetoricians and philosophers, and the doctors and bishops of the Church easily transferred to the basilica the seat from which many of them had given lessons in the schools. It underwent a gradual transformation, its rounded back being flattened and arm rests being provided; in this form it resembled the *solium* or seat of honour of the master of the house.

It was usual to place the bishop's seat on a higher level than those of the presbyters; this was to follow the practice in the civil basilicas where the judge or president sat above the scribes and assessors. The cathedra was thus situated at the centre of the back wall of the apse, behind the altar, and on either side extended the semicircular benches of his assistants, the presbyters. This arrangement, of which there are numerous surviving examples (as at Paros), was thus precisely that described in the Book of Revelation 4. 4–11 where God is on His throne with the elders disposed to His right and to His left.

In the catacombs there are seats cut out of the tufa which were undoubtedly intended for the bishop at the celebration of the liturgy, although some of them are more likely to have been used by catechists.[2] Apart from these a few other early cathedrae have been preserved, notably that of St Gaudosius, which is in the church of Santa-Maria-della-sanita at Naples; this fifth century example is quite chaste in form like the

[1] *H.E.*, vii. 30, 9.

[2] T. Roller, *Les catacombes de Rome*, 1880, II, pl. 63, n. 7, 8.

cathedra of the statue of St Hippolytus, but in time they became more elaborate, like the great throne on which Christ is seated in the apse mosaic of St Pudenziana or like the ivory panelled chair of Maximianus of Ravenna.

The importance of the cathedra lay in the fact that it was the bishop's pulpit, the Jewish custom of remaining seated to deliver the sermon being continued in the Church. The place where the bishop had his cathedra assumed a special dignity in the eyes of the faithful; it was therefore the episcopal church, the official seat of local Christianity, and the building which contained it was, so to speak, of secondary importance, and received the name *ecclesia cathedrae*, i.e. cathedral. Its position at the back of the apse was not however the most convenient and it is likely that use was made of portable cathedrae which could be put near the chancel. St Chrysostom, on the other hand, preached from the *ambon* in the nave in order that the congregation might hear him with greater ease.

The ambon or pulpit was another feature almost certainly taken over by the Christians from the synagogue in which the rabbis employed a kind of desk.[1] Its name derives from the fact that it was ascended (ἀναβαίνειν) by a flight of steps, although sometimes it was called 'the tower' (πύργος) because of its shape. It was from here that the Scriptures were read by the lectors and although before the Peace of the Church there were probably none in use, from the fourth century onwards it became customary to have one or two pulpits in front of the presbyterium. The position of the ambon was not immediately standardized; occasionally it was to be found in the middle of the nave, more frequently to one side of it. Where two ambons were employed, one for the reading of the Gospel, the other for the Old Testament and Epistles, they flanked the choir or presbyterium on either side, and were distinguished by their difference in size and ornament. The lectors usually faced the altar for the Epistle and across the church for the Gospel, but there seems at first to have been no particular side of the altar assigned

---

[1] cf. 1 Esd. 9.42.

to each. Several ambons have been preserved intact,[1] notably those at Ravenna, including one of the sixth century in the Church of St Giovanni Evangelista and one in SS John and Paul dating from 597. These examples are all decorated in a similar fashion, viz. by a series of bands, one above the other, composed of rectangles in which animals and birds have been carved, each creature being confined to one band. In Greece excavations reveal that the ambon passed through three stages of development. At first it consisted of a monolithic pedestal with three or four steps leading up to a rounded platform, e.g. in the Acheiropoetos at Salonika; next it became a semicircular structure with two short flights of steps leading up from the same side to a low platform, occasionally surmounted by a baldachin, e.g.

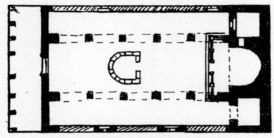

Fig. 31. Church of Kharâb Shems.

basilica A at Thebes; finally, it assumed the form of a high platform, with or without baldachin, approached by two flights of stairs, the one to the east, the other to the west, e.g. basilica B at Nikopolis.[2] The ambon in St Sophia was the fruit of this evolution, belonging to the third type. It was approached by two flights of stairs, one leading from the nave and the other from the eastern apse by a raised passage. According to Paulus Silentarius it was upheld on eight columns, and was flanked by semicircles of more columns of Synnada marble on white bases with gilt capitals. This lavish construction, standing in the middle of the nave, was

[1] No stone ambons have been found in North Africa.

[2] Lemerle, *op. cit.*, pp. 358–61.

[95]

so extensive that the choir was able to take up its position beneath it in an enclosure formed by a breast-high balustrade of Hierapolis marble slabs placed between the columns. Not entirely unlike this disposition were the exedrae, of which traces of at least fifteen have been found in Syria.[1] In many churches it was usual to have a horse-shoe shaped construction a little to the west of the centre of the nave, of which it occupied in length sometimes a quarter, sometimes as much as a third (*Fig. 31*). It consisted of a low parapet against which on the interior a semicircular bench was placed. In the centre was a baldachin, carried on four columns, above a seat (*Fig. 32*); this was the cathedra which served as the

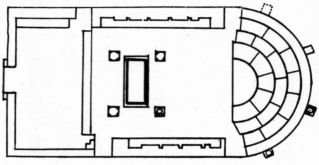

Fig. 32. Exedra, Rosafa-Sergiopolis.

ambon or pulpit for the bishop when he addressed the congregation.[2] His presbyters and lectors would occupy the bench and it is likely that the choir also, as in St Sophia, had its place within this enclosure. It is evident that where this plan was adopted there would be no synthronus in the apse, and the first part of the Eucharist would take place in the midst of the nave, the clergy proceeding to the altar for the remainder of the service after the dismissal of the catechumens. The episcopal throne was probably made frequently of wood, which would account for its total

[1] Lassus, *Inventaire*.

[2] A similar construction has been found in church XI at Al-Hirāh in Mesopotamia.

disappearance from many buildings, but one example in stone has been found at Bennaoui, some forty miles to the south-east of Aleppo. Carved out of basalt, its sides grooved to enable it to be fixed into place, the back and arms are so steeply inclined that the seat is little more than a narrow ledge; the rear is ornamented with a scroll pattern and a cross; an inscription provides its date: A.D. 500[1]

To all this splendid furniture was added as a setting the mosaics adorning the apse and the walls, and the highly coloured pavements on which, as there were no pews, the faithful stood with outstretched arms for prayer and sat for the sermon.[2] Just as the wall mosaics were frequently the offering of rich princes and bishops, so the poorer members of the church paid for sections of the floor, their gifts being still recorded by numerous inscriptions.

[1] R. Mouterde in *Atti del III Congresso internazionale di archeologia cristiana*, 1934, p. 469.

[2] In Africa and Gaul however, it was the custom as late as the fifth century to stand for both sermons and lections.

V

ADJOINING BUILDINGS

OUTSIDE THE CHURCH the most noticeable feature, apart from the impressive porticos, was the *cantharus* which stood in the centre of the atrium. The word κάνθαρος designates a two-handled drinking vessel with a deep bowl on a single foot; it was also made in a large size and as such served to catch the water which poured from a fountain and so it came to be known as a *phiale*. When adopted by the Christians it was placed in the forecourt[1] and used for the symbolical purification of those who were about to enter the church, usually by the washing of their hands, as the following inscription from Bieda (Blera) in the province of Viterbo records:

	XPIA		NE	
LABAMA		NVS	ET	ORA
	VT	REMITTANT		

i.e. *Christiane lava manus et ora ut remittant (tibi peccata)*.[2] The column on which this is incised obviously supported a cantharus.

The fountain was generally supplied with spring water by an aqueduct, but Paulinus of Nola had to depend upon rain water which he collected from the roof of his church.[3] Paulinus of Tyre was more fortunate and Eusebius describes his structure in glowing words: 'he hath left a space exceeding large between the temple and the first entrances, and adorned it all around with four transverse colonnades,

[1] Usually in the centre, but there are some interesting exceptions to this, *vide* Lemerle, *Philippes*, pp. 316–18.

[2] Cabrol, II, col. 1,956.   [3] *Ep.*, xxxii. 11f.

fencing the place into a kind of quadrangular figure, with pillars raised on every side, and rising to a convenient height; and in the midst thereof he hath left an open space where men can see the sky, thus providing it with air bright and open to the rays of light. And here he has placed symbols of sacred purifications, by erecting fountains right opposite the temple, whose copious streams of flowing water supply cleansing to those who are advancing within the sacred precincts.'[1]

At Rome the most interesting cantharus of which there is evidence is that which stood in the atrium of St Peter's. Although additions were made to it by Symmachus (498–514) it probably dated back to the reign of Constantine and was partly constructed of material taken from the mausoleum of Hadrian. Eight porphyry columns supported a roof of gilded bronze on which were placed peacocks and dolphins, beneath it, enclosed by marble chancels, each with a griffin carved on it, was a huge bronze pine cone from which the water fell into a square basin.

Where there was no atrium, as was not uncommonly the case in the East, the fountain was placed in the vestibule. On one of the apse mosaics of St Vitale at Ravenna there is a representation of one of the forms these reduced canthari used to take. It consists of a single fluted column surmounted by a classical capital, which in turn supports a bowl, the jet of water springing up from the centre of it. It has been argued that this is the prototype of the holy water stoup of the Middle Ages, but examples of these stoups from the fourth century onwards were already in use in Syria[2] and at Gerasa.[3]

For many centuries churches have been isolated buildings, comprising within one large room all that is necessary for the liturgical life of the community. It would however be a mistake to imagine that this represents an invariable practice and, in particular, that when the church emerged from the private house it made a definite break with all that had taken place there, discarding, as it were, the additional rooms and

[1] *H.E.*, x. 4.   [2] Butler, *Churches*, p. 216.   [3] *Gerasa*, p. 180.

adopting instead one single hall, the basilica. On the contrary there is considerable evidence that the house of God, the *domus Dei*, was only a part of the greater house, the *domus Ecclesiae*. Not only do early documents give the lie to the theory that the church was transformed from a complex to a simple edifice,[1] but archaeological research has shown that the church remained a house into which the basilica was inserted to replace the principal room where the liturgy had been celebrated. Accordingly it must be recognized that the basilica, while being certainly the most important, was not the only part of the architectural complexes erected by the faithful in the first centuries of the Christian era. At Salona in Dalmatia,[2] at Timgad and Tipasa in North Africa,[3] at Gerasa in eastern Palestine[4] and in all parts of Syria[5] these constructions, which earlier expeditions had neglected through lack of time, labour and money, have been excavated and examined in recent years. In many instances these buildings were grouped around a court, although it should be emphasised that this was not the atrium in the sense of an entrance court in front of the west door of the basilica. The precise use of each separate annex is not always easy to determine in default of inscriptions or other indications, but certain of them may be classified beyond reasonable doubt.

There was of course the clergy house where the leaders of the Christian community could live, eat and sleep. There was also a hostelry, πανδοχεῖον, where travellers could find shelter for the night; in Syria, e.g. adjoining the cathedral at Brad, this took the form of a large room divided into two by a row of feeding troughs for the animals, these troughs were separated from each other by upright flag stones on which beams were placed to support a partition. In some towns even baths were supplied in order that Christians might

[1] *Test. Dom.*, trans. in *Gerasa*, p. 175; *Cod. Theod.*, IX. xlv. 4.

[2] F. Gerber, *Forschungen in Salona*, I, 1927.

[3] J. Gagé, 'Nouveaux aspects de l'Afrique chrétienne', *Annales de l'École des Hautes-Etudes de Gand*, I, 1937, pp. 195ff. J. Lassus, 'Autour des basiliques chrétiennes de Tipasa', *Mélanges*, XLVII, 1930, pp. 222ff.

[4] *Gerasa*, pp. 175–80, 265–94.   [5] Lassus, *Sanctuaires*, pp. 22–40.

cleanse themselves without being exposed to the temptations of the public ones; so bishop Placcus erected some at Gerasa in 454–5, comprising *tepidaria*, *calidaria* and a swimming pool in the court, and others have been found at Djemila in North Africa.[1] A fourth annex was used as a *diaconia* or almonry where the deacons distributed charity to the poor and needy. Next to the cathedral at Gerasa there was also a room set apart for the 'choristers of the second class'. Other buildings were used as monuments and tombs, e.g. St Peter's, Rome, and even the baptistery, which to-day is usually nothing more than a font inside the church doorway, was a separate construction with its own special adjuncts.

In the Apostolic and subapostolic ages baptism appears to have taken place in a river or lake, and even in the sea[2], nor is there any substantial evidence of special buildings for the rite before the Peace of the Church. The Pre-Constantinian basilicas may possibly have had baptisteries beside them but the only one of which there is mention is that adjacent to the new church at Tyre, which, built by the voluntary donations of the congregation under the care of the Bishop Paulinus, was dedicated in September 314. In the panegyrical oration which was then delivered, probably by Eusebius himself, the speaker refers to the 'chambers and buildings . . . for those who still have need of cleansing and sprinkling with water and the Holy Spirit.'[3]

The internal arrangement of baptisteries in the West was similar to that of the *frigidaria* in the Roman public baths. The plan was usually octagonal, occasionally circular, with an inner octagon of eight columns which surrounded the sunken font and supported a dome. These columns were united either by architraves or more occasionally by archivolts. The earliest remaining example is the Lateran Baptistery (*Fig. 33*), also known as St Giovanni in Fonte, which is said to have been built by Constantine for the baptism of his sister and his daughter. To it Sixtus III (432–40) added the eight porphyry columns still *in situ* and Hilary (461–8)

[1] H. Albertini, *Atti del III congresso di arch. grist.*, 1934.

[2] Justin, I *Apol.*, lxi; *Recog. Clem.*, VII. xxxviii.   [3] *H.E., loc. cit.*

provided it with a group of annexes at the same time as reconstructing it, adhering however to the original plan. From the Constantinian period also dates St Costanza which, although employed as a mausoleum, was either originally or shortly after its construction used as the baptistery of the neighbouring basilica of St Agnese.[1] From the fifth century there is the Orthodox Baptistery at Ravenna

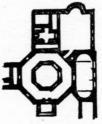

Fig. 33. The Lateran Baptistery, Rome.

and some fifty years later the Arian Baptistery, each of which follows a similar plan.

In the East round buildings were not commonly employed for baptisteries, and even the hexagonal plan at Dêr Sêtā is unusual; the most popular form was that of a rectangle, sometimes broken by a small apse, and in Palestine the quatrefoil was widespread. In North Africa, similarly, a square or rectangular building was common, although there are some interesting exceptions, notably the basilicas at Castiglione, which has its font in a crypt beneath the altar, at Guoéa, where the font occupies the centre of a small chamber flanking the apse, and at Tigzirt where the quatrefoil appears again.[2]

In both East and West the font was habitually sunk below the level of the floor and the steps leading down to it

[1] A. L. Frothingham, *The Monuments of Christian Rome*, 1908, p. 29.

[2] Whereas the church architecture of North Africa is in general uninspired, the baptisteries display considerable initiative and experiment. Thus we find, in addition to the above, the Greek Cross, hexagon and octagon, and, a plan peculiar to Tunisia where at least six examples are known, a central basin spreading out into six or eight branches, thus forming *alveoli* where several candidates could receive baptism simultaneously, e.g. at Sidi Mansour.

symbolized the descent of Christ into the Jordan. Equally the descent into the water symbolized and effected the sacramental union of the believer with Christ in His death on the cross, the catechumen was 'buried therefore with him through baptism into death' (Rom. 6. 4). From this many writers have assumed that baptism was originally by total submersion, but the archaeological evidence all points to immersion with affusion as the normal practice.[1] Examination of those frescoes in the catacombs which represent baptism and of the same scene on sarcophagi and engraved glass reveals no attempt to depict submersion; affusion is indeed shown, and the figures are usually naked, but the water only reaches to their ankles and there is no suggestion that the candidate plunges below the surface. It is moreover difficult to see how he could have done so in view of the shallowness of those fonts which have survived. The majority average from 2 to 4 feet in depth[2] and any possibility of lying down is excluded by the insufficient diameter, e.g. the font at Guoéa which is only eighty centimetres in diameter and one meter in depth, while the baptistery at Khirbit il-Khaṭîb in Syria, dating from A.D. 532, has only a small basin in a deep semicircular niche, both niche and basin being carved in the thickness of the wall.

The method employed for baptism, as the arrangement of the baptistery itself, was analogous to that of the public baths. In the frigidaria at Rome, the water was shallow and the bathers stood upright either in the flow from a projecting spout or pouring it over themselves. In the Lateran Baptistery Constantine placed on the rim of the font a golden lamb from whose mouth a stream of water gushed forth; the parallelism is obvious and leads to the conclusion that the officiant either guided the catechumen's head under the water or directed the flow on to his head with a vessel; this latter practice is evidenced by the design on a spoon from Aquileia of the fourth or fifth centuries which shows a figure

[1] *vide* C. F. Rogers, *Baptism and Christian Archaeology* in *Studia Biblica et Ecclesiastica*, V.

[2] That of St Sophia, 4 feet 6 inches, is the deepest known and is exceptional.

holding a *patera* in the stream of water over the head of the candidate.[1] Where no fountain was provided the patera alone would suffice. It must however be admitted that the Pauline comparison of baptism with burial does suggest submersion, but the burial rites of the ancients were not the same as those in vogue to-day. When a body was laid to rest in the earth, the essential feature of the rite was the casting of a few handfuls of earth upon the corpse,[2] hence the sprinkling of water on the candidate by affusion would appear to fulfil the essentials of comparison with burial. The archaeological evidence therefore strongly suggests the conclusion that submersion was not the original practice of the Church, but came to be thought the correct mode at a later age when infant baptism had become the prevalent custom, and so by the ninth century submersion was commanded (Council of Chelsea, 816, canon 11).

Since the candidates had to disrobe for the ceremony, a dressing room became a necessity and Cyril of Jerusalem is witness to the division of the baptistery for this purpose.[3] More important was the providing of a room where the ceremony could be completed, since it was for centuries the practice of the Church to baptise and confirm at the same time; baptism and confirmation forming one united rite of Christian initiation.[4] This took place on Holy Saturday immediately after the reading of the Twelve Lessons, as a fourth-century inscription from Chiusi witnesses when it records how the deceased, a child, died before receiving the sacrament while the fifth lesson was being read.[5] The chamber designed for the rite was known as the *consignatorium;* the words *consignare* or *consignatio* appear on numerous inscriptions referring to confirmation, e.g. one found at Spoleto dating from the pontificate of Liberius (352–66).[6] At Salona in Dalmatia there is preserved a whole complex of these rooms; to the north of the fifth-century basilica is an

[1] Rogers, *op. cit.*, Fig. 22, p. 267.
[2] Sophocles, *Antigone*, ll. 246, 256; Aelian, *Var. Hist.*, v. 14.
[3] *Catech. Mystag.*, i. 2; ii. 1.
[4] *vide* A. J. Mason, *The Relation of Confirmation to Baptism*, 1891.
[5] C.I.L. XI, n. 2551. [6] De Rossi, *Bull. di archeol. crist.*, 1869, pp. 22-6.

octagonal baptistery, with a consignatorium adjoining it on the west; this is a rectangular chamber, paved with a mosaic representing harts drinking at a fountain, and to one end of it there is the throne where the bishop sat for confirmation; access is obtained to the church by means of a staircase leading up into the narthex.[1] To the east of the baptistery

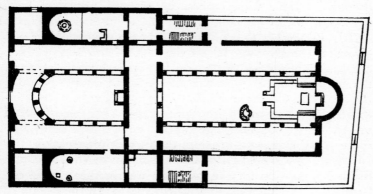

Fig. 34. Basilica A, Thebes.

there is a third small room which is similar to the *pistikon* attached to the baptistery of the martyrium of St Babylas at Antioch. The name pistikon, which is attested by a mosaic found *in situ*, would appear to designate the room where the catechumens recited the creed immediately prior to the actual baptism. A similar tripartite disposition is to be noted at St Theodore's, Gerasa, while other examples of consignatoria with apses are to be seen at Morsott and Tipasa in North Africa and at Ivenna in the valley of the Illyrian Drave. At Thebes, adjoining the atrium of the fifth-century basilica A, there is yet another instance: the first of three rooms is a pistikon entered from the narthex, the second is a consignatorium with bishop's throne, the interesting feature of which is the hollowing out of the arms to make scallop-like containers for the holy oil used for unction, and the third, with an apse at one end, contains the font (*Fig. 34*).

[1] J. Zeiller, *Origines chrétiennes de la Dalmatie*, 1906, pl. 1; but contrast Lemerle, *op. cit.* pp. 340-4.

A further testimony to the unity of baptism and confirmation is given by the words which Ennodius of Pavia places in the mouth of Rome: *Ecce nunc ad gestatoriam sellam apostolicae confessionis uda mittunt limina candidatos; et uberibus, gaudio exactore, fletibus collata Dei beneficio dona geminantur.*[1] From this it is evident that it was the practice for the neophytes, dressed in their white robes, to proceed from the font, *uda limina*, to the *gestatoria sella apostolicae confessionis*. This is clearly a reference to confirmation; hence the candidate was led, after the baptism, before the bishop who administered confirmation in front of the seat of Peter which was kept in the baptistery. The presence of the chair in the Vatican baptistery in the second half of the fourth century is confirmed by a Damasian inscription: VNA PETRI SEDES VNVM VERVMQVE LAVACRVM.[2] The funeral eulogy of Siricius, the successor of Damasus, provides the further information that FONTE SACRO MAGNVS MERVIT SEDERE SACERDOS. Thus although the usual position for the cathedra was in the apse of the basilica, after Damasus, the cathedra to which the bishop of Rome owed his title of *sacerdos magnus* was by the *fonte sacro*.

Since it was the office of the bishop to confirm and since confirmation and baptism were for centuries united, baptisteries were at first usually built only in the episcopal cities, although a few other towns possessed them in order to spare the candidates too long a journey. The permission to have them was however exceptional and Gregory Nazianzus records how many Christians advanced as an excuse for delaying baptism the length of the journey to the nearest baptistery.[3] Until baptism and confirmation were finally separated this scarcity of baptisteries continued and it was not until the eleventh century that every parish possessed one of its own. In the East on the other hand, where from an early date the priest was allowed to confirm in place of the bishop, employing for the purpose oil which had been episcopally blessed, baptisteries were much more numerous and were by no means confined to episcopal centres. In parts of

---

[1] *Apologet. pro synodo*, P.L., t. LXIII, col. 206.
[2] Cabrol, III, col. 41.   [3] *Orat.*, XL, *De Sancto Baptismo*, 27.

XIII. Exterior of apse, church at Ḳalb Lauzeh

XIV.   Font at Dura-Europos

Syria by the sixth century nearly every town had its baptistery, not infrequently two and sometimes apparently three.[1]
The multiplication of baptisteries was carried out apace in
the West after the emphatic teaching of St Augustine on the
doctrine of original sin had led to a great increase in the
number of infants baptized. There are indeed numerous
inscriptions from the first centuries referring to children, but
none of them record that they were baptised. Many epitaphs
from the fourth and the first half of the fifth centuries indicate
the persistence of the tendency to postpone baptism as long
as possible; these are those which speak of the departed as
neophytes, a word applied to the recently baptized. Particularly worthy of note is this epitaph from Bologna:

```
HIC REQVIESCVNT
DVO FRATRES INNO
CENTES CONSTANTIVS
NIOFITVS QVI VIXSIT
ANNIS OCTO MH D . VI
DEPOSITVS III ID NOB
CONS DD NN ARCADI
ET HONORI AVGG .
IVSTVS FIDELIS QVI
VIXIT ANNIS VII[2]
```

From this it is apparent that the elder was baptized
in extremis dying while still a neophyte; his younger brother
survived him by over a week and so had the title of *fidelis*.

[1] Butler, *op. cit.*, p. 204.   [2] Cabrol, XII, col. 1,105.

VI

THE GEOGRAPHICAL
DISTRIBUTION

CHRISTIAN ARCHITECTURE naturally differed from country to country and, in certain areas where the native population was virile and creative, even from district to district. The geographical distribution of the several types of church building used by Christians in the the first six centuries of our era have already been partly described in considering their origins, but in order to complete the survey a general account of Christian architecture as it appears in each country is necessary.

PALESTINE[1]

Although Palestine was originally the fountain-head of Christianity, the majority of the population turned deaf ears to the proclamation of the Gospel, so that, as stated above,[2] it was not until the fifth century that the country as a whole became Christianized. Consequently there were few, if any, churches before Constantine beautified the Holy Places with his munificent gifts.

The commonest form in Palestine was a long basilical building, with a nave and side aisles; indeed nine tenths of the Churches followed this plan, there being only one basilica with rectangular transepts and very few with a trefoil east end. The semicircular apse was almost invariably inscribed, St Theodore at Gerasa, the foundation of which was laid in 494, being a notable exception. In the fourth-century churches the aisles are narrow and the apses small, but in the following century, with the growth of the worshipping community, the aisles were enlarged to the breadth of half the

[1] J. W. Crowfoot, *Early Churches in Palestine*, 1941.   [2] *vide* p. 3.

nave and the chord of the apse was similarly increased to the full width of the nave. The prothesis and diaconicon, an habitual feature of the Hellenistic basilica, which flanked the inscribed apse frequently took the shape of side apses, e.g. in the Church of SS Peter and Paul at Gerasa, c. 540. The exterior of these buildings was very plain, although atria were not uncommon, and the earliest narthex is not to be found before the reign of Justinian. In the interior, mosaics were used lavishly and the floors were decorated with tessarae cut from the native tinted limestones. The main roofing material was wood, of which there was a sufficient local supply, but the marble that was used had to be imported, although some of it was pillaged from earlier buildings.

In most Palestinian churches the chancels are long and deep, occupying in some as much as a third or even a half of the nave, above which they were raised by one or two steps. The altar stood on the chord of the apse beneath a ciborium, the cathedra and the seats of the presbyters being placed behind in the usual fashion. There are however one or two basilicas in which a different arrangement has been adopted, e.g. the Propylaea church at Gerasa in which the cathedra is placed on the chord of the apse and the altar has been moved further west, the seats for the presbyters being placed on either side of the altar in blocks facing each other, a characteristic of many Greek churches. The ambon or pulpit was practically part of the chancel and was usually on the south or epistle side.

The earliest Palestinian churches were not congregational but memorial buildings and they were built according to the centralized plan. These were the foundations of Constantine —the Holy Sepulchre, the Church of the Nativity and the Church on the Mount of Olives.

The Anastasis, or the Church of the Holy Sepulchre, was dedicated in the year 335, having taken ten years to build. Eusebius has given a description of its arrangement, but unfortunately it is not free from ambiguity. According to him the complex of buildings consisted of (1) 'the sacred cave' decorated with columns; (2) a space enclosed on three sides with porticos; (3) a basilica, the interior of which was floored with marble slabs of various colours and the exterior shone with polished stone; the panelled ceiling was overlaid with gold and the roof was covered with lead; (4) on either side of the basilica were two colonnades, the outer row consisting of columns, the inner of square pillars; the gates were placed at the east end to receive the multitudes entering the church; (5) opposite the gates was the 'hemisphere' 'which rose to the very summit of the church'; this was encircled by twelve columns, the number of the Apostles, surmounted by silver bowls; (6) before the church was the atrium, surrounded by porticos and beyond its gates the open market-place.[1] There is nothing to be gained by discussing at length all the possible interpretations of this account, rather let it suffice to state what is the most probable. The principal buildings were set out axially on a long line running from east to west.[2] A great entrance at the east end led into the atrium, out of which three doors opened into a five-aisled basilica, later called the Martyrium. Beyond this was a second court, at the south side of which stood the rock of Calvary. Finally at the end of the line was the Anastasis, the hemisphere, which is the word used by the Silentiary of the dome of St Sophia.[3] This building had a wooden dome, with an outlet to the sky, and enshrined the holy tomb which was encircled by twelve columns.[4] The whole edifice was destroyed by Chosroes II of Persia in 614, only the rotunda being restored. It is however

---

[1] *Vita Const.,* iii. 34–39.

[2] W. Harvey, *Church of the Holy Sepulchre,* 1935. This disposition, although differently orientated, was imitated at Gerasa in the plan of the Fountain court group of buildings, J. W. Crowfoot, *Churches at Jerash,* p. 36.

[3] W. R. Lethaby, *Mediaeval Art,* 1912, p. 28.

[4] This reconstruction has been questioned by E. Dyggve (*Gravkirken i Jeru-salem, Konstantinske problemer i ny belysning,* 1941). He argues that the basilica Anastasis was not the rotunda but a hypaethron in which the sepulchre of Christ was to be found. It was an open court with porticos, one of which was rounded to envelop the tomb, itself decorated with columns. It is indeed possible to interpret the St Pudenziana mosaic in this way, Christ being seated in the basilica Anastasis, his throne occupying the place of the tomb. The rotunda, which according to this theory would be later than Constantine, was simply constructed by closing the circle, already partly in existence, with the wall and semicircular colonnade which formed one of the sides of the Constantinian hypaethron.

figured on a fifth-century ivory in the British Museum, on the mosaic floor at Madaba and on the apse mosaic of St Pudenziana at Rome. It is probable that the last also represents one of the rites which took place at Jerusalem and which have been described by Etheria, when the bishop sat on his throne in front of Calvary with his deacons grouped around him in a circle.

In the right hand corner of the Pudenziana mosaic there is also a representation of the Church of the Holy Nativity, constructed by Constantine at Bethlehem. The atrium is depicted as a long low building with a lofty porch, the taller edifice in the centre is the basilica and on the left there is a still loftier octagon. Apart from the crenellation on the basilica and the small building in the mid-background this is probably a faithful reproduction of the general scheme, which was therefore set out axially as at Jerusalem and consisted of an atrium, a five-aisled basilica and an octagonal chapel above the grotto.[1] According to Eutychius, writing in the tenth century, this church was replaced by a larger one at the orders of Justinian, and there seems sound reason to accept his testimony. The present sixth-century building is also a five-aisled basilica, crossed by transepts, the north, south and east arms all terminating in apses. The church is 160 feet long and under the crossing is the cave in the rock.[2] There is no evidence that there was an altar in the original building, but neither was there one in the Anastasis, for they were planned not for liturgical purposes but for evidential considerations, that all might see the places where the Christ was born and buried and rose from the dead.

Near to the traditional place of the Ascension on the Mount of Olives above the cave where Jesus was believed to have instructed the apostles in the Last Things, there was at the time of Constantine a three-aisled basilica, preceded by an atrium. At a slightly later date a centralized building

[1] W. Harvey, *Structural Survey of the Church of the Nativity*, 1935; E. T. Richmond, 'On the Church of the Nativity', *The Quarterly of the Department of Antiquities of Palestine*, V, 1936.

[2] R. Weir Schiltz, *The Church of the Nativity at Bethlehem*, 1910.

open to the sky, either round or polygonal, was erected over
the rock which was supposed to bear the print of our Lord's
feet. Still extant at the end of the seventh century it was seen
and described by the French pilgrim and bishop Arculfus.

Other centralized buildings have already been mentioned,
such as the cathedral at Bosra, 512–13, of which St John's at
Gerasa was a reduced edition. This last had a basilica on
either side, one dedicated to St George in 529, and the other
to SS Cosmas and Damianus in 533; all these opened on to
a common atrium.

In general the Palestinian churches may be described as
unoriginal in conception, which in view of the comparatively
late date of the extension of Christianity to the native population is not surprising. The Constantinian churches are,
however, an exception and it is probable that in them
oriental builders, working from Asiatic and Hellenistic
architectural forms, first solved the problem of the relation
between the circumscribing aisles and the interior arcades
which bore the dome. Both the authority of Constantine and
the growth of the practice of pilgrimages to the Holy Places
would ensure their exerting a wide influence, so that this
type became well known throughout the Christian world.

Syria

To the north in Syria there is an abundance of remains,
and indeed in no other country of the world have the monuments of antiquity been preserved in such perfect condition
and in so many varieties. From the seventh century village
after village was left completely deserted, and the strength of
the original buildings, together with the absence of any
attempt to reconstruct them, ensured their continuance to
the present day. As a consequence the early Christian
architecture of Syria has received considerable attention,
and the researches of Melchior de Vogüé in 1861–2, the
Princeton expedition under H.C. Butler between 1894 and
1910 and, more recently, the investigations of Jean Lassus
have provided a wealth of important material.

[112]

One of the most salient factors in the study of Syrian architecture is the geological formation of the country; local materials had a great effect on the processes of construction, so that the buildings fall into distinct groups dependent upon the type of stone available and whether or not there was a convenient supply of wood.

In northern Syria, a limestone region, where the rock was near the surface and easily quarried, it was natural that a freestone architecture should develop; the blocks were cut to the specified size in the quarries which were often opened up near the site of the proposed church, being transformed into cemeteries or cisterns after they had served their purpose. Since the countryside was thickly wooded a double pitched timber roof covered with tiles was employed as a protection against the heavy winter rains. From the outset the normal type of building was the Hellenistic basilica which would appear to have been adopted not as the consequence of local experiments—it is in fact not a native creation at all—but under the direction of the clergy, influenced no doubt by the architecture of the capital Antioch. The oblong plan, with longitudinal columnar supports for the clerestory, and a semicircular apse between side chambers at the east, continued in use from the fourth to the sixth century, the only variety being in the number of bays and entrances, and in the proportion between the central nave and the side aisles; thus the fourth-century church of Khârab Shems (*Fig. 31*), that at Mshabbak which dates from *c.* 460, and the South church at Bānḵûsā (*Fig. 35*), a sixth-century building, are all examples of essentially the same arrangement. A tendency towards elaboration should however be noted which found expression partly in the increased use and diversity of architectural ornament and moulding, and partly in the stone construction being extended up into the roof. This latter feature is particularly evident in the sixth-century Bizzos church at Ruwêḥā where the longitudinal supports take the shape of the letter T, the front of which is directed towards the centre of the nave and is extended up into the clerestory to carry high transverse arches. A further variant in secondary details also calls for special mention, viz. the placing of entrance doors in the south wall alone which is found in numerous churches of the fourth and of the beginning of the fifth centuries. Strzygowski suggested that this disposition was in order to facilitate the lighting of the building,[1] while

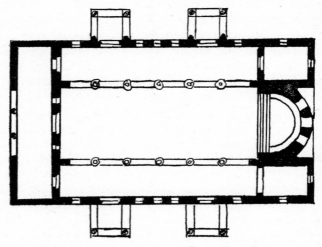

Fig. 35. The South church, Bānkûsā.

Leroux considered it to be a compromise between the Hellenistic and the transverse oriental basilicas,[2] but Bernheimer, in a careful survey, has adequately refuted these theories[3] and argues instead that these 'round-the-corner-rooms', as he styles them, derive from a type which was known in Mesopotamia in the fourth millenium B.C. and had a continuous history down to the temple of Bel at Palmyra in the first century A.D. While admitting this influence it is also to be remarked that the basilica was not an independent unity but was part of a complex with which it had therefore to be set in intimate relationship, accordingly

[1] *L'art chrétien de Syrie*, p. 101.

[2] 'Les églises syriennes à portes laterales', *Mélanges Holleaux*, 1913, p. 123.

[3] 'An Ancient Oriental Source of Christian Sacred Architecture', *A.J.A.*, XLIII, 1939, p. 648.

the importance of local domestic architecture should not be underestimated. A two column porch for each portal or a continuous colonnade along the full length of the wall were usual in these early churches, but when in the sixth century the western entrance became normal the narthex was adopted.

Alongside the Hellenistic basilica in north Syria there was a second group of buildings; these were simple rectangles, with a sanctuary divided off at the east end, occasionally by a pair of columns carrying an architrave from wall to walls, more frequently by an arch. These chapels, which probably originated from the small pagan temples of similar plan which are not uncommon in the region, seem to have influenced the basilica in the sixth century, since at least eighteen churches are known in which the semicircular apse has been rejected in favour of a rectangular sanctuary (*Fig. 36*).

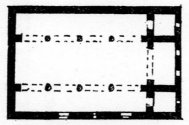

Fig. 36. Church of Khirbit Ḥasan.

The Hauran or southern Syria is a basalt region, and the extreme hardness of this lava had a profound effect upon the local architecture. The width of any single room was determined entirely by the maximum length, usually about ten feet, to which the flagstones composing the roof could be cut. While quite sufficient for the private house, in which the rooms could be spanned by the stones laid from wall to wall, this was by no means adequate for a church, and therefore the expedient was adopted of joining together a number of these narrow rooms, the walls being pierced by arches. The width of the building then became dependent upon the

[115]

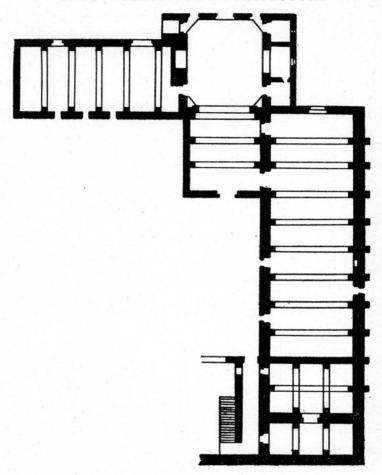

Fig. 37. The Ḳaiṣarîyeh, Shaḳḳā.

span of the arch, while its length could be extended in-
definitely by the multiplication of these units; it is obvious
that the flagstones would then be lying along the length of
the building from arch to arch. This procedure was used in
the pre-Christian period and is seen perfectly exemplified
in the third-century palace or Ḳaiṣarîyeh at Shaḳḳā (*Fig. 37*).

XV. Interior of church at Ṭafḥā, looking towards apse

The disproportion of this building however also reveals the main fault of this method, viz. that it was still only possible to increase the size of the room in one direction, the width remained fixed by the span of the arch; a further development therefore took place, and it is to be seen in the basilica at Shakkā which is of the same period as the palace. This was achieved by placing three oblong rooms side by side, the centre one being put into communication with those flanking it by the piercing of its walls by further arches. This

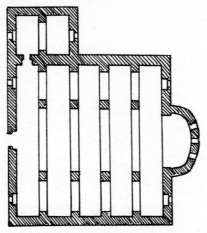

Fig. 38. Church of Ṭafḥā.

basilica therefore consists of a nave separated from the side aisles by two rows of low square piers. These piers supported first, transverse arches across the nave; secondly, longtitudinal arches; thirdly, two transverse arches, one above the other, one spanning the side aisle and the other the gallery above it. The crown of the upper arch reaches to the level of the crown of the nave arch. Christian architects followed these different types exactly, the church of Julianos (fourth century) at Umm-i-Djimal reproducing that of the Kaisarîyeh and the church at Ṭafḥā (fifth century) that of the basilica at Shakkā (*Fig. 38*). The so-called Hauran style was therefore derived exclusively from pagan prototypes which in turn were mainly the outcome of conditions imposed by the nature of the local stone.

In the course of time the desire for uniformity and the influence of northern Syria combined to introduce the Hellenistic basilica into the south. At first the architects attempted to reproduce the classical plan while adhering to the processes of construction with which they were familiar— the church of Klaudianos is a late example of this at Umm-i-Djimal—but this was not an adequate assimilation and so wood and tiles were imported which enabled the erection of buildings with double pitched roofs and clerestories in exact imitation of the normal type. At the same time the adoption of the tripartite sanctuary in the sixth century marked the final triumph of the general model. This brief survey of the architecture of southern Syria may be brought to a close by noting that side by side with the hall churches in the Hauran style, and with the imported Hellenistic basilica, there were also a few buildings of the transverse oriental type and two main examples of the domed central plan, viz. the cathedral at Bosra (512–13) and the church of St George at Zor'ah (515) (*Fig. 20.*)

North eastern Syria is also a black basalt area, but here the influence of Antioch on the one side and of Mesopotamia on the other has prevented the creation of any native style, as in the Hauran; instead the Hellenistic basilica with foundations of basalt, upper courses of clay or sundried brick and a timber roof is everywhere to be found. There is indeed some variety in disposition, and some churches have an extra arch added at the west end on either side to form a kind of interior narthex by means of a high transverse arch thrown across the nave, but the plans conform to a single general type, apart from a few churches of the central plan, e.g. the domed basilica at Ḳaṣr Ibn Wardân, 564 (*Fig. 24*).

All churches in Syria have certain things in common— the sanctuary at the east end: the division of the building into at least two main parts, the nave and presbyterium, and the triumphal arch spanning the opening between these two. While these main features were constant, in other respects there was considerable diversity, so that e.g. in one area alone there would be churches with protruding apses, those with inscribed apses and those with a tripartite sanctuary. This testifies not only to native ingenuity but also to the strength of Christianity throughout the country; nor does the relative scarcity of churches in the fourth century contradict this latter statement, since this was certainly due not to villages remaining pagan but to the paucity and poverty of the inhabitants of the countryside. In the fifth and sixth centuries, on the other hand, the country enjoyed an era of great economic prosperity through its rapidly expanding export trade in oil and wine; towns developed, villages increased in size and farms sprang up in all parts; the Church, too, benefited materially, and through the generosity of local landowners it was in a position to provide centres of worship wherever there was a demand. The Persian conquest of 610–12 and the Mohammedan victories of 633–38 led to the abandoning of district after district, but the ruins remain to provide an important chapter not only in the history of Christian architecture but also in the story of the steady advance of Christianity throughout Syria from the fifth to the seventh centuries.

Mesopotamia and Armenia

From the previous description of the four principal types of basilica, it will be recalled that one form in Mesopotamia was that with the transverse plan, an indigenous creation, influenced by both Egyptian and Babylonian architecture. Reference has already been made to the church of St Jacob at Salah;[1] other examples include the church of the Virgin at Khakh, with transverse nave covered by a dome buttressed by semi-domes, and that of St James at Nisibis, A.D. 350–65, which consists of three contiguous rooms each in three parts with small apses in the thickness of the wall.

The *Hallenkirche* was another indigenous type, and a number of single-naved churches with entrances in the south

[1] *vide supra*, p. 50.

wall indicate the tenacity of the ancient round-the-corner disposition. The churches of the Tūr Abdīn, which form a compact and uniform group, are of this kind, consisting of a single rectangular nave, orientated east-west, with a semi-circular apse at the east end and a narthex occupying the full length of the south side. Apart from the apse, this plan derives directly from Assyrian and Babylonian temples.[1] At Ctesiphon there is clear evidence of the influence of the Sassanid palaces in a church of the fourth century. It is an oblong room, with a row of pillars inside along the north and south walls; the entrances are lateral; at the east end there are three rectangular spaces, the centre one of which serves as the sanctuary. Some hundred miles to the south of Ctesiphon, at Al Hirāh, two churches of the sixth century (numbered V and XI) reveal unmistakable Syrian influence; there the entrances are again lateral, the sanctuary rect-angular, with side chambers.[2]

Despite these last two examples, it would be incorrect to suppose that the Mesopotamian architects displayed no originality, native initiative is very much to the fore, and though the Hellenistic basilica penetrated the country in the fourth century it had no widespread vogue.[3]

Armenia, the first state to adopt Christianity officially, has a profusion of architectural types but with a marked predilection for the dome. The earliest extant monuments of the fifth and sixth centuries are for the most part basilicas with barrel vaults, e.g. the church at Erenik', built at the end of the fifth century, and that at Eghivard erected by the Catholicos Moses (574–604). This however was an alien type and disappeared from Armenia as soon as Greek and Syrian influences waned; henceforth the centralized plan carried all before it.

Apart from the church at Awan, built by the Catholicos John of Bagaran (590–611), there are few examples of the

---

[1] U. Monneret de Villard, *Le Chiese della Mesopotamia*, 1940.

[2] D. Talbot Rice, 'The Oxford Excavations at Hira,' *Antiquity*, VI, 1932, pp. 276–91.

[3] M. van Berchem and J. Strzygowski, *Amida*, 1910. There is however a domed basilica at Meiafarqin, dating from A.D. 591.

domed unit before the seventh century at the earliest, but the variety of plans and the complexity of the structures of these later surviving examples indicate that they were not initial attempts, and much originality must be accorded the Armenian Christians.

The churches were all built of smooth stone with a rubble concrete core; they were usually small but presented a solid mass on the exterior which rarely reflected the basic plan. The apse and the adjoining chambers were often built in the thickness of the walls, and the dome, frequently covered with a pyramidal or conical roof, rested on a polygonal or cylindrical drum. Vigorous sculptured designs, consisting of crosses, interlaced motifs and even animal and human figures, in low relief, decorated the outside walls, while around the drum of the cupola were blind arcades with slender coupled colonnettes; in this respect the Armenian churches are to be contrasted with the majority of other Western Christian buildings which were more restricted in their external ornamentation.[1]

Asia Minor

The early Christian architecture of Asia Minor falls into two main groups, within the second of which, however, there is considerable variety; the character of these groups is determined by their geographical position, the first being found along the littoral where Hellenistic influence was all-predominant, the second belonging to the hinterland where native genius contributed to a diversity of forms.

In the coastal areas, with which may also be included the islands of Lesbos and Samos, the Hellenistic basilica was almost the exclusive type. The atrium was customary, although there are four basilicas on the islands which have little or no trace of them, and the narthex was habitual, exceptions being the basilicas at Miletus and Perga in

[1] J. Strzygowski, *Die Baukunst der Armenier und Europa*, 2 vols., 1918; A. Fetvadjian, 'An outline History of Armenian Architecture', in *The Journal of the Royal Institute of British Architects*, XXIX, 1922, pp. 585–94; Sirarpie Der Nersessian, *Armenia and the Byzantine Empire*, 1945.

Pamphylia. The number of entrances, however, was not stereotyped, e.g. there were two in the basilica near Smyrna and three in those at Miletus and Perga. Three aisles were universal and the apse was usually inscribed,[1] an exception to this being the basilica at Pergamus in Mysia. Side chambers, *pastophoria*, were provided in almost all instances, in the form of oblong rooms adjoining the apse with occasionally small apses at one end, e.g. at Corycus in Cilicia (*Fig. 39*).

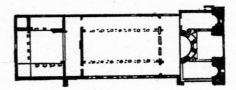

Fig. 39. Church of Corycus.

Two interesting variants of this disposition are the basilica at Miletus, in which space at the sides and rear of the apse is provided by elongating the walls of the aisles and then joining them together behind the apse by a sweeping arc, and the basilica at Perga, which in addition to side chambers has a form of transept. The altar seems to have been placed in front of the apse, although this is not always certain, and fenced with cancelli stretching directly across the nave from colonnade to colonnade.[2]

The architecture of the coastland was largely derivative, drawing its main inspiration from Greece via the islands of the Aegean, but the pressure of the East is seen in the adoption of the tripartite sanctuary and the consequent inscribed apse. Further influence from the same quarter is evident in the domed basilica, and here Constantinople too must certainly have had its part to play. At Ephesus the earlier Hellenistic basilica, in which the Ecumenical Council met in A.D. 431, was replaced by a brick cross-domed

[1] It is because the apses of the basilicas on Lesbos and Samos are all inscribed that they are included here and not in the survey of Greece, where the apses were all protruding.

[2] All the basilicas mentioned hitherto belong to the fifth century.

basilica; the domed basilica spread along the coastal plain and is to be found in the fifth century at Myra and Trabala in Lycia and then, moving up the valleys, it appeared at Khodja Kalessi before 451 (*Fig. 23*), and in Meriamlik by A.D. 470, finally extending even as far as Galatia, where at Ancyra there is a domed basilica dating from the fifth to the seven centuries, and at Yurme there is another example of the fifth century.

In Lycaonia the basilica appears widely in two forms, the true basilica and the barn church or *hallenkirche*, but in Cappadocia, on the other hand, it is almost unknown, and the cruciform predominates even for congregational use, e.g. the fifth-century church of the Forty Martyrs at Skupi. The cross-shaped plan, almost always the *crux commissa*, was employed all over the central plateau, and many examples are to be found in southern Lycaonia, to the north of the Taurus range in the Kara Dagh.

The Kara Dagh is an island of volcanic mountains, its highest peak being Mahaletch, at the north foot of which there is a valley with the ruins of an ancient city called by the inhabitants Maden Sheher, and by the people of the surrounding country Bin Bir Kilisse. The general characteristics of its architecture are sufficiently distinctive to be easily summarized: stone was the main building material, brick being only employed for decoration; with very rare exceptions the vault and the dome were the sole method of roofing; the atrium was non-existent but the narthex was an invariable feature.[1] This narthex was of a stereotyped plan and consisted of an entrance chamber, communicating with the nave by a door, and of two outer chambers laid against this one, on either side, that to the south being walled off and unapproachable except from the aisle, that to the north having an arch (*Fig. 40*). The façades frequently have upper storeys, to the right and left of the main door, and towers reminiscent of ancient Hittite constructions; other entrances were not uncommon in the side walls. The altar was placed

---

[1] W. M. Ramsay and G. L. Bell, *The Thousand and One Churches*, 1909, pp. 302–3.

in the first bay of the nave in front of the apse, which protruded, and it was screened from the rest of the church either by wooden rods hung with draperies or with stone slabs decorated with crosses on the side facing the congregation. The horseshoe arch was prevalent, there being eight

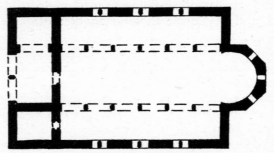

Fig. 40. Church No. 3, Bin Bir Kilisse.

examples of an apse with horseshoe ground plan in the churches of the basilical type in the Kara Dagh; the same shape was also used for windows, a number of which lighted each aisle.

Amongst the cruciform buildings in this area one of the most noticable is the large church at Mahaletch—the side chambers west of the transepts do not affect the structural conception (*Fig. 41*). It is connected by a narrow stone passage leading from the exo-narthex with a memorial chapel of the Greek cross type standing to the north west; another passage from the narthex connects the complex with the monastery.

Round and octagonal forms were well known to the architects of Asia Minor, but the pendentive is rare; the corbel and squinch, the Inner Asiatic forms of dome setting, prevailing. The fifth-century church at Derbe in Pamphylia is an example of the round plan and at Cassaba in Lycia there are several octagons, a plan which St Gregory of Nyssa so strongly recommended in his letter to Amphilocus. Particularly worthy of note is church No. 8 at Bin Bir Kilisse which combined both octagon and cruciform (*Fig. 42*).

[124]

This second group of buildings, those of the central plateau, is by no means subservient, as those on the littoral, to Hellenistic influence; the details are worked out freely by local builders deriving their inspiration from the architectural traditions of Asia.

GREECE

In Greece, the home of the megaron and the naos, the basilica was in extensive use from the early Christian period.

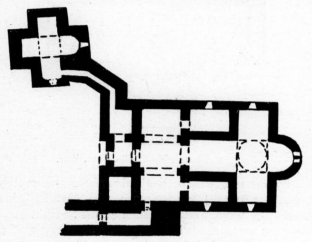

Fig. 41. The great church, Mahaletch.

Excavations during the past three decades have brought to light some twenty to thirty examples which range from Macedonia in the north to the Gulf of Corone in the south, all of them having marked similarities. The projecting apse is invariable and is usually raised above the main floor of the church, being left vacant except for the bishop's throne which stands against the rear wall in the centre. The altar, a little way into the nave in front of the three steps leading up into the apse, is often surmounted by a ciborium, as in the basilica B at Thebes and in the great basilica at Nikopolis. The banks of seats for the presbyters are disposed on either

[125]

side of the altar, facing each other across it, e.g. in Thebes A and B, in the basilica at Stobi and in that of Doumetrios at Nikopolis.[1] The sanctuary is extended into the body of the

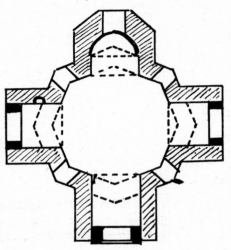

Fig. 42. Church No. 8, Bin Bir Kilisse.

church by cancelli which, beginning from the presbyters' seats, run for several yards inside and parallel with the columns of the nave, and then turn across at right angles to them to form an entrance in the centre. When the synthronus is situated in the apse itself, as in the basilica at Sicyon, the cancelli start directly from the arms of the apse and then turn inwards in the usual fashion. Three aisles are the norm, although there are at least two known exceptions to this, viz. the basilicas at Nikopolis and Epidaurus, each of which has five. There are several instances of large ambons, placed at approximately the centre of the length of the nave just to one side near the southern colonnade, e.g. Thebes A, Nikopolis and Stobi. An interior narthex is universal, and an atrium

[1] This 'rectangular' disposition was superceded in the sixth century by the more widespread semicircular arrangement, with cathedra and synthronus around the back of the apse; the change was probably due to the desire not to interrupt communication with the pastophoria, rendered more important by the rite of the prothesis. At Olympias both rectangular and semicircular are found.

with porticos and phiale is frequent. Entrance from the atrium into the narthex is by means of two doors, opposite the side aisles, there being seldom a third central doorway as in the West, although the church of St Demetrius (A.D. 412–13) at Salonika has one. Following the usual plan of the Hellenistic basilica, as it is known elsewhere, tribunes over the side aisles, supported by archivolts, are habitually provided for women.

To those basilicas already listed,[1] all dating from the fifth century, may be added Philippi A, the Acheiropoetos at Salonika and those at Dium and Dordona. The last three, however, have certain peculiarities: neither the Acheiro-poetos, which has an exo-narthex, nor the church at Dium has traces of any cancelli, while the basilica at Dordona has

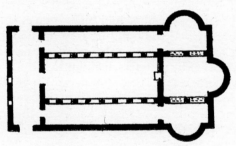

Fig. 43. Church of Dordona.

apses let into the side walls of each aisle at the sanctuary end, so that they face each other across the altar and form a kind of transept and, since it has three doorways instead of the usual two, western influence may be suspected[2] (*Fig. 43*). But apart from these, the basilicas are remarkably alike and to describe one is to draw attention to details common to the majority.

[1] G. A. Soteriou, Χριστιάνικη καὶ Βυζαντίνη Αρχαιολογία, τόμ. Α', 1942. I am grateful to Miss K. Pappayanopoulou for calling my attention to this work, which contains plans and full descriptions of all the buildings referred to in this section.

[2] Lemerle, *Philippes*, pp. 376–7, suggests that it is the result of the fusion of a triconcha and the rectangular basilica.

Basilica A at Thebes in Thessaly was built during the course of the fifth century (*Fig. 34*). The front wall of the complex had a tower at each corner and three doors leading into the atrium, which had covered porticos on three sides, that immediately in front of the principal entrance being rounded. At the other end of the open central space, against the façade of the church, was the phiale, an unusual position for it to occupy, as it was customary to place it in the middle of the atrium. On either side were adjoining rooms, consisting of a baptistery, a consignatorium and a pistikon on the north[1] and a vestry on the south. Two doors opened into the narthex and two further corresponding doors communicated with the side aisles, the nave being separated from it by two columns, thus emphasizing the distinction between the church proper where the faithful were gathered, and the porch where the catechumens and penitents had their place. Two rows of nine columns divided the building into nave and side aisles, there being a pulpit in the centre of the nave. A small gate between two slender pillars surmounted by an arch and pediment gave access to the sanctuary which was enclosed with marble cancelli, perforated slabs between low posts. After turning through two right angles so that they finally run parallel with the colonnades, the cancelli came to an end against the presbyters' seats, which were arranged in two banks on either side and approached by three steps. In between these, in front of the apse, stood the altar, probably beneath a ciborium reared on four columns. Behind the altar, three steps led up into the raised apse at the back of which was the cathedra, the bishop's throne, the whole was enclosed within walls which merged into those of the adjoining buildings on either side of the atrium. Two doors in the boundary wall behind the apse were probably used by the women to reach the staircase situated to the north and south of the west end of the church, by which they mounted to the tribunes over the side aisles.

Although the centralized plan was destined to prevail eventually in Greece, domed buildings only gradually

[1] *vide supra*, p. 105.

became common, and then principally in the form of the domed basilica. Thus basilica B at Philippi, dating from the third quarter of the sixth century, reveals the influence of St Sophia, Constantinople, while the Church of Our Lady of the Hundred gates in Paros,[1] also of the sixth century, was a cross-domed basilica, its baptistery following the same plan, and marking an advance upon the old church, in the form of a simple basilica which it still contains in its north east corner. In the same period the tripartite sanctuary began to make its appearance, e.g. in St Titus at Gortyna in Crete. Of round churches, however, there are few examples; there is indeed St George at Salonika, but this was originally a pagan building before it was adapted for Christian use.[2] There can be no doubt that the basilica persisted with great tenacity and it was not until the eleventh century that the great building of Byzantine churches in Greek lands took place.

EGYPT AND LOWER NUBIA

The glories of Egyptian architecture under the Pharaohs were not perpetuated in the early Christian buildings; instead native inventiveness seems to have spent itself, and, as in North Africa, there was little more than the production of styles and features created elsewhere.

The basilicas fall into two main groups, differentiated not by their plan but by the material from which they were constructed. The first group consists of those built under imperial patronage, e.g. the basilicas of St Menas at Maryūt of the fourth and fifth centuries; for these prefabricated columns, capitals and beams were imported from the Greek islands and from Constantinople. The second group consists of those churches erected by the natives themselves, either of masonry pillaged from ancient Egyptian temples, e.g. the chapel of the White Monastery at Sohag, or of plain bricks,

---

[1] H. H. Jewell and F. W. Hasluck, *The Church of Our Lady of the Hundred Gates in Paros*, 1920.

[2] *vide supra*, p. 53.

e.g. the chapel of the Red Monastery which, like its companion, is of the fifth century.[1]

Cutting across this classification by material is that by plan, and here two main types are to be noted: those churches revealing Syrian and Mesopotamian influence, with side entrances either on the north or south, and those of the Hellenistic type with entrance in the western façade.[2]

The sanctuary was either rectangular or semicircular, side chambers appearing almost invariably.[3] Galleries were customary above the side aisles, and a narthex was formed by returning the columns of the nave across the west end. Despite the high cost of wood it was used for roofing, although in the south, where it was very scarce, brick tunnel vaults were employed.

The dome enjoyed a wide vogue, and it was not uncommon to have a cluster of three or more surmounting each building. Three doors in the western façade were customary, but there was no atrium—the church being directly on the street. The cruciform plan was unknown, but square churches with a small dome placed approximately at the centre appeared later, e.g. at Edfu, the Deir Melak Mikhail.

The majority of the constructions were timid, awkward and fragile, and the lack of native originality is further revealed by their unsuccessful efforts at sculptural ornament; this however was in part balanced by the use of paintings and frescoes, e.g. the realist school of portraiture at Fayum and the frescoes at El Bagauat.[4]

Since it was not until c. A.D. 540 that Christian missionaries sent by Justinian and Theodora reached Nubia its architecture falls mainly outside the period of this study, but a brief reference may be made to its principal features. As

---

[1] A. Badawy, *Les premières églises d'Egypte jusqu'au siècle de saint Cyrille*, 1947.

[2] U. Monneret de Villard, 'La basilica cristiana in Egitto', *Atti del IV congresso di archeologia cristiana*, I, 1940, pp. 291–319.

[3] Examples of a trefoil sanctuary are to be found in the Red and White Monasteries.

[4] Somers Clark, *Christian Antiquities in the Nile Valley*, 1912.

in Egypt, so in Lower Nubia the basilica was adopted, but since it was usually of two storeys there was no clerestory. The sanctuary or Haikal with apsidal end was inscribed, and was separated from the body of the church by a wall with an arched opening. The two side chambers which flanked it were sometimes connected by a corridor behind the apse. Entrance into the basilica was commonly by doors in the north and south aisles. Despite the influence of Justinian the centralized plan was not popular, and the dome was merely an incident in roofing, not the determining factor of the whole complex.[1]

NORTH AFRICA

The names of Tertullian, Cyprian and Augustine are them-selves sufficient evidence of a thriving Christianity in North Africa extending over several centuries. It is not surprising therefore to find that the religious edifices were to be counted in their thousands, although today there are only the ill-preserved remains of some two or three hundred. So prolific was the building that in Numidia, for example, it was not unusual to find several basilicas in one small village although its population could never have been very great.[2] As a consequence of this profusion the construction was mediocre and although there were exceptions such as the basilicas of Tebessa and Tigzirt, there was little of high artistic value. The types were mainly derivative; there was no original work and little attempt was made to solve architectural problems, rather these seem to have been carefully avoided. Most of the churches were built of rubble with chain courses of freestone, the use of brick being rare; the materials were in the main taken from pagan buildings, but were used with such lack of discrimination that where columns were of unequal length pillaged capitals were inserted as bases, e.g. as at Guelma, to bring them up to a uniform level.

[1] G. S. Mileham, *Churches in Lower Nubia*, 1910.

[2] In part this was due to the Donatist schism.

The basilical plan was almost universally adopted;[1] three aisles, separated by columns or pillars, were the norm, but to this there were exceptions, the basilica at Orléansville having five, and that at Tipasa at first seven and later nine (*Fig. 44*). Archivolts carried the clerestory on which the roof

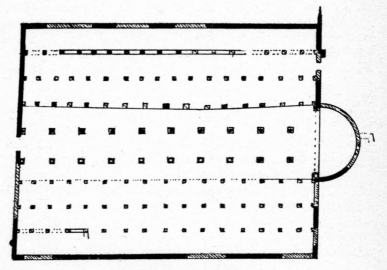

Fig. 44. Church of Tipasa.

was placed; this was probably of wood since despite the lack of remains the thickness of the walls precluded vaulting. There were some rectangular sanctuaries but more commonly there was a deep semi-circular apse, either projecting or inscribed, usually flanked by side chambers in the Syrian fashion. In Numidia and proconsular Africa, the southern chamber is usually closed to the nave but open to the apse, while that to the north is closed to the apse but open to the nave; in Zeugitana and Byzacium, on the other hand, where side chambers are equally widespread, there is no known example of this disposition. The altar was occasionally

[1] L. Leschi, 'La basilique chrétienne en Algérie', and A. G. Lepeyre, 'La basilique chrétienne de Tunisie', in *Atti del IV congresso internazionale di archeologia cristiana*, I, 1940, pp. 145–67, 168–244.

placed in the apse, but more usually in the nave. Occasionally a kind of chancel consisting of a single (as at Bérian) or a double (as at Tipasa) colonnade separated the presbyterium from the nave; elsewhere low walls were employed. A portico, with inclined roof supported on pillars, shaded the three doors in the western façade; there were in addition frequent examples of a vestibule or narthex and also of additional secondary entrances in both north and south walls.[1] The doorways were surmounted by straight lintels, bearing the sacred monogram or a dedicatory inscription, above which there was a lunette formed by the semicircle of an arch pierced with windows.

From this brief outline it will be evident that although North Africa had very close ties with Rome, architecturally it was independent of her; the Latin basilica had no direct influence and, indeed, many of its principal features were unknown. Thus no examples of transepts have been found, nor should the wings of some prolonged side chambers, as in the basilica at Guesseria, be mistaken for them. Atria were very rare, only three being known for certain, at Tebessa, Henchir Tikoubaï and Bir-Knissia, while the architrave was entirely absent. The use of inscribed apses, side chambers and narthexes, the adoption of galleries over the aisles in the fifth century and the occasional appearance of rectangular sanctuaries all point to Egypt and Syria as the mainspring of North African architecture. This eastern influence did not, however, lead to any widespread use of the centralized plan; the dome was completely absent from Mauretania and Numidia, but in Tripolitania Justinian was responsible for the erection of five domed basilicas at Leptis Magna, and also for another at Carthage itself.[2] A few trefoil chapels were also built, including one annexed to the large church at Tebessa.

[1] cf. M. Simon, 'Fouilles dans la basilique de Henchir el Ateuch (Algérie),' *Mélanges d'arch. et d'hist. de l'école de Rome*, 1934, p. 125. This basilica has a west end, other examples of which are known, consisting of an unbroken wall closing in the narthex which is entered by doors at its northern and southern extremities.

[2] cf. C. Diehl, *L'Afrique byzantine*, 1896, pp. 420–6.

In addition to the Hellenistic basilica there were also numerous single nave buildings, either dedicated to the apostles, *memoriae apostolorum*, or to martyrs, *memoriae martyrum*; there were indeed so many of them that the Council of Carthage in 438 considered it necessary to restrict their number (canon 34). These were in the form of a rectangle with an apse at one end, of which the diameter was usually, though not always, equal to the width of the building. There are traces of cancelli in some, e.g. at Bir Ben Zireg and Henchir Bou Ghadaine, and some of them had lateral

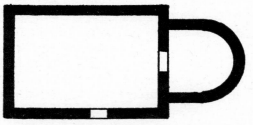

Fig. 45. Chapel of Announa (Thibilis).

entrances thus conforming to the 'round-the-corner' type (*Fig. 45*) and providing a further indication of African dependence upon the East.

ITALY

It is natural in a review of early Christian architecture in Italy to begin with Rome, where there are not only many churches surviving intact, but where there are the traces of many more revealed by excavation. Reference has already been made to the two principal round buildings, St Stephano Rotundo, probably a transformed pagan edifice, and St Costanza (A.D. 324–6)[1] and a description has been given of the old St Peter's with its five great aisles and its transepts. Also dating from the fourth century is the basilica of St Pudenziana rebuilt in the time of Siricius (384–99), best known for its magnificent apse mosaic of Christ enthroned, a topographical picture of many of the Constantinian buildings

[1] *vide supra.*, p. 53.

in Jerusalem itself. Apart from the mosaic its most interesting feature is the segmental apse which as far as is known was never again employed. The original basilica of St Maria Maggiore was built between A.D. 420 and 430; it consisted of a nave and two aisles, with an apse immediately joining the nave; the transepts and apse of the present church are of the thirteenth century.[1] Excavations have also recovered the original plans of many other churches, in particular that of St Lorenzo in Lucina. This building was given its present form in 1606, but it has now been established that its fifth-century predecessor was one of the largest and most important Roman churches of the period; its measurements corresponding exactly with those of St Sabina. It had two aisles and a nave lighted by thirteen windows, and ended in a stilted semicircular apse, the fore-choir of which was accompanied at least on the right by a side room continuing the aisle.[2]

The influence of Rome outside its immediate vicinity is difficult to assess, certainly to the south at Nola Paulinus (353–451) followed an independent course in planning his basilica to adjoin that of St Felix. It had an *apsis trichora*, i.e. a group of three apses, the principal one of which he pierced with arches opening on to a covered court with the earlier basilica on the other side. In order to orientate his church to his satisfaction in relation to the older building, he had the entrance at the east, although he admitted that this was contrary to 'the more usual custom.'[3] At Naples, the Basilica Severiana (367–87) had an apse similarly pierced with openings.

Equal with Rome in the importance of its buildings is Ravenna, the seat of the imperial government after the fall of the capital. Here *c.* 450 the tomb of Galla Placidia was erected[4]

---

[1] R. Krautheimer, 'Recent Publications on St Maria Maggiore in Rome', *A.J.A.*, XLVI, 1942, pp. 373–9.

[2] R. Krautheimer, 'Recent Discoveries in Churches in Rome', *A.J.A.*, XLIII, 1939, pp. 388ff. Brief descriptions are also given of the churches of SS Nereo et Achilleo, St Lorenzo in Fonte, St Maria de Metrio, St Petronilla in Domitilla, and St Susanna; *vide* also the same author's *Corpus Basilicarum Christianarum Romae*, I, 1937.

[3] *Ep.*, xxxii 13.   [4] *vide supra*, p. 76.

(*Fig. 29*), a cruciform building which had been preceded at Milan by St Ambrose's basilica, also cruciform, and was contemporary with the church of SS Peter and Paul, now Sant' Abondio, at Como. The great church of St Vitale (526–47) has already been considered in full,[1] but it may be noted further that its influence spread to Milan, where the fifth-century St Lorenzo Maggiore reproduced the octagon encircled by an aisle with galleries.[2] Ravenna was a great centre of eastern and Byzantine conceptions, and the basilicas of St Apollinare Nuovo, *c.* 500, together with the nearby St Apollinare in Classe, 538–49, were both Hellenistic, with the usual protruding apse, polygonal at the exterior, and narthex. Opposite to Ravenna, across the Adriatic in Istria, another Hellenistic basilica is also to be found at Parenzo; its cathedral, although rebuilt, preserves the plan of the sixth-century original. The two side aisles end in apses sunk into the outer walls and the nave leads up to a deep apse, polygonal at the exterior. There is no narthex but a large atrium stands in front of the façade, opposite to which, on the other side of the court, is an octagonal baptistery, an arrangement employed as long ago as the fourth century in the cathedral of Aquileia. At Grado, in the sixth century, there is evidence not only of Hellenistic influence, in the cathedral which, unlike Parenzo, has a narthex, but also of Syrian, for the church of St Maria has the tripartite sanctuary common to so many of the eastern churches of that century. This eastern penetration was indeed to increase throughout Italy to produce the Lombardic style of which so many fine monuments remain to the present day.

GAUL AND SPAIN

Since it was not until the second half of the fifth century that Gaul became substantially Christian, it is not surprising that the most ancient archaeological evidence of church building only dates from the beginning of that century with Cassian's

---

[1] *vide supra*, p. 58.
[2] G. T. Rivoira, *Lombardic Architecture*, 1910, I, p. 72; P. Verzone, *L'Architettura religiosa dell'alte medioevo nell' Italia settentrionale*, 1942, pp. 79–91.

basilica at Marseilles[1] and then in the form of an inscription at Minerve, now in the museum at Narbonne, which speaks of a basilica erected by the Bishop Rusticus.[2] The side walls of the nave of St Pierre at Vienne probably date from the same period, while from the following century there is the round church of St Germain-l'Auxerrois at Paris. The buildings of the Merovingian period, some of which were of wood, did not survive the political unrest of the times and but for the literary evidence little would be known of the general character of the architecture. From Gregory of Tours, however, it is evident that the basilica was the norm, there being numerous spacious examples, such as those at Clermont and at Tours, the latter, dedicated in honour of St Martin in 470, having a tower and belfry; while the basilica built by Patiens, Bishop of Lyons, in the same year, in honour of the popular Gallic saint Justus, had a magnificent atrium adorned with Aquitainian marbles, the ceiling of the church was gilded, the windows were of green glass and the walls were apparently covered with mosaics.[3]

In Spain scarcely any buildings have survived from the period before the invasion of the Visigoths in A.D. 456. Only three are of real interest, and the first of these is the basilica of San Pereto near Manacor, which had three aisles and a western atrium complete with fountain. At Gavia La Grande near Granada there is the remains of a baptistery which is partly underground and consists of a barrel-vaulted corridor leading into a square domed chamber. The episcopal palace at Merida follows the plan of the Roman house with rooms opening on to an atrium. Two of these rooms are oblong and terminate in apses, the smaller contains a font and the larger, since it has frescoes of white robed priests, was probably a chapel.

Visigothic buildings have not been preserved in large numbers, and of those which were not destroyed many were

---

[1] *Vide supra*, p. 33.

[2] C. Enlart, *Manuel d'archéologie française*, 1927, I, p. 116.

[3] Sidonius, ii. 10; for a list compiled from the literary sources, *vide* R. de Lasteyrie, *L'architecture religieuse en France à l'époque romane*, 1912, pp. 37ff.

so reshaped by the Mohammedans as to bear little resemblance to their original form. The most common plan was that of the Greek cross inscribed, but the only building which can be placed with certainty in this period is San Miguel de Tarrasa in Catalonia, and even then it is impossible to be more precise than to say that it was erected between A.D. 450 and 693. It was originally the baptistery of the basilica of Egara; externally a square with projecting polygonal apse, internally it had the angles rounded, and the apse in the shape of a horseshoe. In the centre was a square font with eight columns rising from it, carrying the groined vaults and central cupola.

As for Gaul, there is literary evidence for a thriving Spanish Christianity, albeit beset by the vicissitudes of Arianism, but archaeology can add little to the picture to be drawn from the written sources.[1]

CONCLUSION

Even from this cursory survey of the early Christian churches throughout the different countries one factor clearly emerges, viz. the immense variety of plans. There is of course, even amidst such diversity, a certain similarity, since the buildings were destined for the same use—the celebration of the Liturgy—but this did not prevent the burgeoning of native genius, and the creation of new types went on apace.

Together with the development of architecture there was also that of ornament; here too the ebb and flow of influences, the importance of trade routes and pilgrimages, the impetus of political events and conquests all contributed to the enrichment of the churches' splendour. Splendour, indeed, is not too emphatic a word, for the carved capitals, balustrades and lintels, the shimmering mosaics adorning the apse and the nave walls, the marble pavements, the fine hangings and the vessels of precious metal could only produce the most profound effect upon the individual believer, intensifying his awareness of sharing in the very worship of heaven itself.

[1] Bernard Bevan, *History of Spanish Architecture*, 1938.

GLOSSARY

ABACUS: upper member of column supporting beam or arch.
AGORA: forum, public place.
ALAE: small rooms flanking tablinum.
AMBON: pulpit.
AMBULATORY: place for walking.
APSE: semicircular construction roofed with half dome.
ARCHITRAVE: beam.
ARCHIVOLT: arch springing from column.
ARCOSOLIUM: recessed tomb with arched space above.

BALDACHIN: canopy.
BEMA: apse; more commonly, space between nave and apse.

CALIDARIA: warm baths.
CANCELLUS: balustrade.
CANTHARUS: fountain.
CARTIBULUM: stone table.
CATARACTAE: perforated plates across shaft communicating with confessio.
CATHEDRA: bishop's throne.
CELLAE CIMITERIALES ⎫ funeral chapels.
CELLAE MEMORIAE ⎭
CHAIN-COURSES: a bond course of stones or bricks fastened together continuously by means of other stones set across them.
CHALCIDICUM: room or porch; an appendage to a civil basilica.
CHANCEL: low partition or wall; space enclosed by low parapet separating the sanctuary from the nave.
CHORD OF APSE: straight line joining the two arms of the arc.
CIBORIUM: baldachin.
CLERESTORY: part of wall of church, with series of windows, above aisle roofs.
COLONETTE: small column.
COLONNADE: series of columns usually supporting flat roof.
CONCHA: apse.
CONFESSIO: tomb of martyr placed beneath altar.
CONSIGNATORIUM: chamber for rite of confirmation.
CORBEL: projection of stone jutting out from wall to support weight.
CUPOLA: dome.

DIACONIA: almonry.
DIAKONIKON: vestry.

L

[139]

DOMICAL VAULT: vault in which uniformly curved surfaces reach down without break into angles of arches.

EXEDRA: a semicircular construction.

FENESTELLA: stone grating closing opening into confessio.
FRIGIDARIA: cold baths.

GYNAECEUM: women's gallery.

HYPAETHRON: building open to air, i.e. without roof over centre.
HYPOSTYLE: room of which roof is supported by columns.

ICONOSTASIS: screen separating sanctuary from main body of church.
IMAGINES CLYPEATAE: ancestral portraits.
IMPLUVIUM: cistern.
INSCRIBED APSE: apse whose semicircular outline is masked externally by a straight wall.

LACUNARIA: panels in the ceiling.

MARTYRIUM: chapel enshrining relics of martyr.
MATRONEUM: part of church reserved for women.
MEGARON: Greek house.

NAOS: temple.
NARTHEX: vestibule incorporated into the body of the church.
NYMPHAEUM: sanctuary of nymphs.

OSTIUM: entrance hall.

PALAESTRA: gymnasium.
PASTOPHORIA: side chambers used for collection of bread and wine prior to Eucharist.
PATERA: shallow dish or saucer.
PERISTYLE: space surrounded by rows of columns.
PERRON: platform in front of door of church, ascended by steps.
PHIALE: fountain.
PILASTER: rectangular column.
PISTIKON: chamber where catechumens recite creed prior to baptism.
PORTICO: colonnade.
PRESBYTERIUM: apse; place occupied by presbyters.
PROPYLON: ante-porch.
PROSTAS: recess in house containing household gods.
PROTHESIS: place for preparation of bread and wine prior to Eucharist.

QUATREFOIL: four-cusped figure, resembling symmetrical four-lobed leaf.

ROTUNDA: building of circular ground plan; dome; circle.

SARCOPHAGUS: stone coffin.
SCHOLA: school.
SIGMA: table in shape of half moon.
SOLEA: choir.
SPANDREL: space between shoulders of adjoining arches.
SQUINCH: series of superimposed arches flung across interior angles of polygon to provide support for dome.
STOA: portico.
STYLOBATE: continuous base upon which row of columns is supported.
SYNTHRONUS: seats for presbyters.

TABLINUM: recess in house containing household gods.
TEMENOS: sacred enclosure.
TEPIDARIA: lukewarm rooms in baths.
TETRAKIONION: monumental doorway.
TRANSENNA: perforated stone plate.
TRANSEPT: transverse part of cruciform church.
TRANSEPT MARTYRIUM: transverse part of church used to provide space around tomb of patron saint.
TRANSEPT PROTHESIS: transverse part of church used for collection of offertory.
TRIBUNE: gallery; apse.
TRICLINIUM: dining-room.
TRICONCHA: building having three apses at one end.
TUFA: rock of rough texture of volcanic origin.

VESTIBULUM: porch.

BIBLIOGRAPHY

Antioch-on-the-Orontes, Publications of the Committee for the Excavation of Antioch and its Vicinity, 1934 onwards.

Atti del III congresso internazionale di archeologia cristiana, 1934.

Atti del IV congresso internazionale di archeologia cristiana, 1940, 2 vols.

A. Badawy, *Les premières églises d'Egypte jusqu'au siècle de saint Cyrille*, 1947.

G. Baldwin Brown, *From Schola to Cathedral*, 1886.

J. Barnea, Τό παλαιοχριστιανικὸν Θυσιαστήριον, Θεολογικὴ Βιβλιοθήκη, No. 5, Athens, 1940.

R. Bernheimer, 'An Ancient Oriental Source of Christian Sacred Architecture', *A.J.A.*, XLIII, 1939, pp. 647-68.

B. Bevan, *History of Spanish Architecture*, 1938.

L. Bréhier, 'Les origines de la basilique chrétienne', *Bulletin Monumental*, LXXXVI, 1927, pp. 221-49.

—— 'Anciennes clôtures de choeurs antérieures aux iconostases dans les monastères de l'Athos', *Studi Byzantini et Neoellenici*, VI. 2. 1940, pp. 93-105.

R. Busquet, *Histoire de Marseille*, 1945.

H. C. Butler, *Architecture and other Arts*, 1904.

—— 'The Tychaion of Es-Sanamein and the plan of early churches in Syria', *Revue Archéologique*, 1906, II. pp. 413ff.

—— *Early Churches in Syria*, 1929.

L. A. Choisy, *L'art de bâtir chez les Byzantins*, 1883.

Somers Clark, *Christian Antiquities in the Nile Valley*, 1912.

K. A. C. Creswell, 'The Origin of the Plan of the Dome of the Rock', *British School of Archaeology in Jerusalem, Supplementary Papers*, 2, 1924.

—— *Early Muslim Architecture*, 1932, 2 vols.

J. W. Crowfoot, *Churches at Jerash, British School of Archaeology in Jerusalem, Supplementary Papers*, 3, 1931.

—— *Early Churches in Palestine*, 1941.

C. Diehl, *L'Afrique byzantine*, 1896.

G. Dix, *The Shape of the Liturgy*, 1945.

Glanville Downey, 'The architectural significance of the use of the words *stoa* and *basilike* in classical literature', *A.J.A.*, XLI, 1937, pp. 194-211.

L. Duchesne, ed. *Liber Pontificalis*, 1886-92.

[143]

E. Dyggve, 'Probleme des altchristlichen Kultbaus, Einige archäologisch begründete Gesichtspunkte zu Grabkult und Kirchenbau', (*Zeitschrift für Kirchengeschichte*, LIX, 1940. pp. 103–13).

—— *Ravennatum palatium sacrum. La basilica ipetrale per cerimonie. Studii sull'architettura dei palazzi della tarda antichità,* 1941.

—— *Gravkirken i Jerusalem, Konstantinske problemer i ny belysning,* 1941.

—— and R. Egger, *Forschungen in Salona,* III, 1939.

M. Ecochard, 'Le sanctuaire de Qal'at Sem'ân', *Bulletin d'Etudes Orientales*, VI, 1936.

C. Enlart, *Manuel d'archéologie française,* 1927, 2 vols.

A. Fetvadjian, 'An outline history of Armenian Architecture', *The Journal of the Royal Institute of British Architects,* XXIX, 1922 pp. 585–94.

A. L. Frothingham, *The Monuments of Christian Rome,* 1908.

J. Gagé, 'Nouveaux aspects de l'Afrique chrétienne', *Annales de l'Ecole des Hautes-Etudes de Gand,* I, 1937, pp. 195ff.

F. Gerber, *Forschungen in Salona,* I. 1927.

A. Grabar, *Martyrium, Recherches sur le culte des reliques religieux et l'art chrétien antique,* 1946, 2 vols.

H. Gregoire, 'Les Baptistères de Cuicul et de Doura', *Byzantion,* XIII, 1938, pp. 589–93.

S. Gsell, *Les Monuments antiques de l'Algérie,* 1901, 2 vols.

H. M. Gwatkin, *Selections from Early Writers illustrative of Church History to the time of Constantine,* 1914.

J. A. Hamilton, *Byzantine Architecture and Decoration,* 1933.

A. Harnack, *The Expansion of Christianity in the first three centuries,* 1905.

W. Harvey, *The Church of the Holy Sepulchre,* 1935.

—— *Structural Survey of the Church of the Nativity,* 1935.

G. de Jerphanion, 'Sur l'église de Saint-Simeon Stylite au Djebel Sem'ân', *Orientalia Christiana Periodica,* IX, 1943.

H. H. Jewel and F. W. Hasluck, *The Church of Our Lady of the Hundred Gates in Paros,* 1920.

E. Junyent, *Il titolo di San Clemente in Roma,* 1932.

S. Keck, 'The Tychaion of Phaena-Mismiyeh', *A.J.A.,* XLV, 1941. pp. 98ff.

J. R. Knipfing, 'The Libelli of the Decian Persecution', *H.T.R.,* 1923, XVI, pp. 345–90.

I. B. Konstantynowicz, *Ikonstasis, Studien und Forschungen,* I, 1939.

C. H. Kraeling, ed., *Gerasa, City of the Decapolis,* 1938.

BIBLIOGRAPHY

R. Krautheimer, *Corpus Basilicarum Christianarum Romae*, I, 1937.

—— 'Recent Discoveries in Churches in Rome', *A.J.A.*, XLIII, 1939, pp. 388ff.

—— 'Recent Publications on St Maria Maggiore in Rome', *A.J.A.*, XLVI, 1942, pp. 373-9.

D. Krencker, *Die Wallfahrtkirchen des Simeon Stylites in Kal'at Sim'an, Ergebnisse von Untersuchungen im Frühjahr 1938, Fortschritte und Forschungen*, 1939.

Sven Larsen, 'A Forerunner of Hagia Sophia', *A.J.A.*, XLI, 1937, pp. 1-5.

J. Lassus, 'Autour des basiliques chrétiennes de Tipasa', *Mélanges*, XLVII, 1930, pp. 222ff.

—— 'Deux églises cruciformes du Hauran', *Bulletin d'Etudes Orientales*, I, 1932.

—— *Inventaire archéologique de la région au Nord-Est de Hama*, 1935, 2 vols.

—— *Sanctuaires chrétiens de Syrie*, 1947.

R. de Lasteyrie, 'La direction de l'axe de l'église est-elle symbolique?' *Bulletin Monumental*, 1906.

—— *L'architecture religieuse en France à l'époque romane*, 1912.

H. Leclerq, *Manuel d'archéologie chrétienne*, I, 1907.

R. Lemaire, *L'origine de la basilique latine*, 1911.

P. Lemerle, *Philippes et la Macédoine orientale*, 1945.

—— 'A propos des origines de l'édifice cultuel chrétien', *Bulletin de la Classe des Lettres et des Sciences Morales et Politiques*, XXXIV, 1948, pp. 309ff.

—— 'Aux origines de l'architecture chrétienne', *Revue Archéologique*, XXXIII, 1949, pp. 167-94.

G. Leroux, *Exploration archéologique de Délos*, II, *La salle hypostyle*, 1904.

—— 'Les églises syriennes à portes laterales', *Mélanges Holleaux*, 1913.

—— *Les origines de l'édifice hypostyle*, 1913.

W. R. Lethaby, *Mediaeval Art*, 1912.

—— and H. Swainson, *The Church of Sancta Sophia, A Study of Byzantine Building*, 1894.

W. Lowrie, *Christian Art and Archaeology*, 1901.

J. Mackinnon, *From Christ to Constantine*, 1936.

R. Martin, 'La Stoa Basileios, Portiques à ailes et lieux d' assemblée', *Bulletin de Correspondance Hellénique*, LXVI-LXVII, 1942-3, pp. 274-98.

A. J. Mason, *The Relation of Confirmation to Baptism*, 1891.

R. L. P. Milburn, 'The Persecution of Domitian', *Church Quarterly Review*, CXXXIX, 1945, pp. 154–64.

G. S. Mileham, *Churches in Lower Nubia*, 1910.

G. Millet, 'L'Asie Mineure', *Revue Archéologique*, I, 1905, pp. 101–5.

U. Monneret de Villard, *Le Chiese della Mesopotamia*, 1940.

Valentine Müller, 'The Roman Basilica', *A.J.A.*, XLI, 1937, pp. 250ff.

Sirarpie Der Nersessian, *Armenia and the Byzantine Empire*, 1945.

A. Parrot, *Malédictions et violations des tombes*, 1939.

N. Pevsner, *An Outline of European Architecture*, 1942.

G. Picard, 'La basilique funéraire de Julius Piso à Mactar'. *Comptes Rendus de l'Académie des Inscriptions et Belles-Lettres*, 1945, pp. 185–212.

—— 'Fouilles de Mactar', *Bulletin archéologique du Comité des Travaux historiques et scientifiques*, Feb., 1947, pp. xx–xxvii.

W. M. Ramsay and G. L. Bell, *The Thousand and One Churches*, 1909.

T. Dayrell Reed, *The Rise of Wessex*, 1947.

D. Talbot Rice, 'The Oxford Excavations at Hira', *Antiquity*, VI, 1932, pp. 276–91.

—— *The Background of Art*, 1939.

E. T. Richmond, 'On the Church of the Nativity', *The Quarterly of the Department of Antiquities of Palestine*, V, 1936.

G. T. Rivoira, *Lombardic Architecture*, 1910, 2 vols.

C. F. Rogers, *Baptism and Christian Archaeology, Studia Biblica et Ecclesiastica*, V.

T. Roller, *Les catacombes de Rome*, 1880, 2 vols.

J. Sauvaget, *Inventaire des monuments de Damas*, 1932.

—— *La mosquée ommeyyade de Médine, Etude sur les origines architecturales de la mosquée et de la basilique*, 1947.

R. Weir Schiltz, *The Church of the Nativity at Bethlehem*, 1910.

A. M. Schneider, *Die Hagia Sophia zu Konstantinopel*, 1939.

R. Schultze, 'Basilika', *Römisch-Germanische Forschungen*, II, 1928.

W. Seston, 'Hypothèse sur la date de la basilique constantinienne de Saint-Pierre de Rome', *Cahiers Archéologiques*, II, 1947, 153–9.

—— and C. Perrat, 'Une basilique funéraire païenne à Lyon', *Revue des Etudes Anciennes*, XLIX, 1947, pp. 139–59.

E. B. Smith, 'The Megaron and its Roof', *A.J.A.*, XLVI, 1942, pp. 99–118.

G. Soteriou, Ἡ πρόθεσις καὶ τὸ διακονικὸν ἐν τῇ ἀρχαίᾳ ἐκκλησίᾳ, Θεολογία περιοδ. Β', τόμ. Α' Athens, 1941, pp. 76-100.

—— Χριστιάνικη καὶ Βυζαντίνη Αρχαιολογία, τόμ. Α', 1942.

BIBLIOGRAPHY

J. Strzygowski, *Kleinasien*, 1903.

—— *Die Baukunst der Armenier und Europa*, 1918, 2 vols.

—— *The Origin of Christian Church Art*, 1923.

—— *L'ancien art chrétien de Syrie*, 1936.

—— and M. van Berchem, *Amida*, 1910.

E. H. Swift, *Hagia Sophia*, 1940.

H. A. Thompson, 'Buildings on the West Side of the Agora', *Hesperia*, VI, 1937, pp. 1–226.

M. A. R. Tuker and Hope Malleson, *Handbook to Christian and Ecclesiastical Rome*, I, 1900.

P. Verzone, *L'Architettura religiosa dell'alte medioevo nell'Italia settentrionale*, 1942.

L. H. Vincent and E. M. Abel, *Emmaus, sa basilique et son histoire*, 1932.

R. Vielliard, *Les origines du titre de Saint-Martin-aux-Monts à Rome*, 1931.

J. B. Ward-Perkins, 'The Italian Element in Late Roman and Early Mediaeval Architecture', *Proceedings of the British Academy*, 1947, pp. 163–94.

W. R. Zaloziecky, *Die Sophienkirche in Konstantinopel und ihre Stellung in der Geschichte des Abedandlandischen Architektur*, 1936.

J. Zeiller, *Origines chrétiennes de la Dalmatie*, 1906.

INDEX